AMERICAN LABOR

FROM CONSPIRACY
TO
COLLECTIVE BARGAINING

MEDIATION, INVESTIGATION AND ARBITRATION IN INDUSTRIAL DISPUTES

George E. Barnett and David A. McCabe

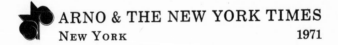
ARNO & THE NEW YORK TIMES
New York   1971

Reprint Edition 1971 by Arno Press Inc.

Reprinted from a copy in
The U.S. Department of Labor Library
LC# 71-156403
ISBN 0-405-02913-6

American Labor: From Conspiracy to Collective Bargaining—Series II
ISBN for complete set: 0-405-02910-1
See last pages of this volume for titles.

Manufactured in the United States of America

MEDIATION, INVESTIGATION, AND ARBITRATION IN INDUSTRIAL DISPUTES

MEDIATION, INVESTIGATION AND ARBITRATION IN INDUSTRIAL DISPUTES

BY

GEORGE E. BARNETT, Ph.D.
PROFESSOR OF STATISTICS, THE JOHNS HOPKINS UNIVERSITY

AND

DAVID A. McCABE, Ph.D.
ASSISTANT PROFESSOR OF ECONOMICS, PRINCETON UNIVERSITY

D. APPLETON AND COMPANY
NEW YORK   LONDON
1916

Printed in the United States of America

PREFACE

This study of Mediation, Investigation, and Arbitration is based on a report submitted in June, 1915, by the writers to the Commission on Industrial Relations. A considerable amount of illustrative material has been added, the statements have been brought down to date, and some revision has been made in the form of presentation, but the argument and the proposals remain unchanged.

It should be understood that the authors alone are responsible for the views here expressed. For convenience in comparison there are added in the Appendices (II–IV) extracts from the Final Report of the Commission, in which are presented the views of the members of the Commission on the matters dealt with here.

The authors wish to express their appreciation of the kindness and courtesy of the many state officials, employers, trade union officers, and other workmen who supplied information for the orig-

PREFACE

inal report. We are pleased to acknowledge our indebtedness to Dr. L. A. Rufener for the opportunity of examining several chapters of his thesis on "The Work of the Massachusetts Board of Conciliation and Arbitration" and for other valuable suggestions as to sources of information in that State.

G. E. B.,

D. A. McC.

CONTENTS

PART I

STATE AGENCIES OF MEDIATION, INVESTIGATION AND ARBITRATION

PART II

NATIONAL AGENCIES OF MEDIATION, INVESTIGATION AND ARBITRATION

CONTENTS

I

STATE AGENCIES OF MEDIA-
TION, INVESTIGATION
AND ARBITRATION

INTRODUCTION

A very large proportion of the American States have made provision in their laws for agencies of mediation, public investigation, and arbitration in labor disputes. For a study of these agencies, however, attention can most profitably be centered on a few states, since the arrangements in other states are merely duplications of these few or else the machinery provided by law is not in operation to any important extent. The present study is based on a survey of the agencies in Massachusetts, New York and Ohio.[1] All three are important industrial states and possess highly diversified groups of industries. Moreover, the present work of the

[1] Since this study was begun the State of Colorado has adopted a law (April 12, 1915) requiring thirty days' notice of proposed changes in wages or other terms of employment and forbidding strikes and lockouts until after a board of investigation appointed by

agencies of mediation, arbitration and public investigation in these states is at least equal in quality to that in the other states and these states present further advantage for the investigator in that they were among the earliest to establish agencies of mediation and arbitration.

Much has been accomplished by these agencies in all three of these states in the way of reëstablishing and promoting industrial peace. As among the three kinds of activities of such agencies, it is clear that up to the present by far the best results have been obtained through mediation. With the exception of Massachusetts, state agencies of arbitration have been rarely used. Public investigation after failure to secure the settlement of a strike or lockout by mediation

the State Industrial Commission has reported its findings on the matters in dispute. This is the first law of its kind in the United States but it has not yet been in operation long enough to give results of value for this study.

4

has also been used sparingly. It has been resorted to very rarely in Ohio, and until the last two or three years in only a few cases in New York and Massachusetts.

The results achieved by the mediators and arbitrators in the states studied strongly support the conclusion that state agencies of mediation, investigation, and arbitration, if properly constituted and properly manned, would be of great service in all the industrial states in preventing the outbreak of strikes or lockouts and in bringing to an earlier conclusion a large proportion of those which they are unable to prevent. This conclusion is confirmed by interviews with many whose difficulties the state mediators failed to compose and who declined to submit the matters at issue to arbitration by existing state boards. These persons naturally emphasized the desirability of having properly qualified persons to act as mediators, investigators or arbitrators. The vital importance of the proper constitution of the agencies as to personnel as well as to powers and duties was otherwise made clearly evident, as will appear at several points in the description of the agencies and their work.

For convenience in comparison, the description of the systems in the three states has been divided into three sections entitled respectively Mediation, Public Investigation, and Arbitration.

I

MEDIATION

In discussing the subject of mediation it will be most convenient to consider first the existing legal provisions for mediation in the three States and the results obtained under these laws. That will be followed by an analysis of the possibilities of state mediation under proper agencies as evidenced by the experience of the existing agencies. A plan for the constitution, manning, and operation of a state agency of mediation, which, the results of this study indicate, is the plan most likely to lead to the realization of the possibilities of service open to a state agency of mediation, will then be outlined and explained.

MEDIATION AND ARBITRATION

The Mediators.—In Massachusetts the law provides that the State Board of Conciliation and Arbitration shall exercise the function of mediation. The board consists of three salaried persons appointed by the Governor. One member must be an employer or selected from an association representing employers, and one must be selected from a labor organization. The third member is nominated by the other two if they are able to agree upon a third within a specified time. As a matter of fact, they always have been able to agree. The board has a permanent secretary, who, in addition to his other duties, often acts as a mediator for the board.

The Ohio machinery for conciliation and arbitration, until 1913, was the same as that of Massachusetts, except that the members of the board did not receive an annual salary

but were paid at the rate of five dollars a day
when acting for the board, and that one of
the members of the board acted as secretary.
The act creating the Industrial Commission
of Ohio, adopted in 1913, abolished the State
Board of Arbitration and Conciliation, and
conferred upon the Industrial Commission
the duty and power of promoting voluntary
arbitration and mediation. The law provides that the commission shall designate a
deputy to be known as chief mediator and
may detail other deputies to act as his assistants. In November, 1914, the commission
assigned its chief statistician to serve also as
chief mediator. Assistant mediators have
not yet been specifically appointed, but two
members of the staff of the Division of Statistics have in several cases acted in that capacity.

In New York the function of mediation is
intrusted to a chief mediator and his assist-

ants, who are appointed by the Industrial Commission. Prior to the recent law establishing an Industrial Commission (effective May 22, 1915), the chief mediator and his assistants were appointed by the Commissioner of Labor. Under the new law the functions formerly discharged by the Commissioner of Labor have been taken over by the Industrial Commission and general supervision of the work of the Bureau of Mediation and Arbitration is assigned to one of the members of the commission. The chief mediator is also the third deputy commissioner, instead of second deputy commissioner of labor as under the old law. Otherwise the law remains unchanged. The chief mediator is still in immediate charge of the Bureau of Mediation and Arbitration and, as for several years past, has four assistants. One of these has the title of industrial mediator and two that of assistant mediator.

The fourth is a special agent attached to the bureau.

When Mediation Occurs.—In Massachusetts the board is obliged by law to offer mediation when notified by either party, or by the local authorities, that a strike or lockout is seriously threatened or has actually occurred. It intervenes as a matter of course in many other cases. In fact, over half its interventions are made without previous official notification. Its policy is to attempt to mediate in all cases of importance coming to its knowledge. The New York law requires that an officer or agent of the Bureau of Mediation "shall, if practicable, proceed promptly to the locality" in which the strike or lockout is threatened or has occurred and "endeavor by mediation to effect an amicable settlement of the controversy." No strike or lockout involving a considerable number of men goes on for more than a few days without an offer of mediation from the bureau, if the bureau learns of the trouble —and a serious disturbance would not escape its knowledge long. In Ohio, the present law does not specify when mediation shall be offered. The mediators have acted in very few disputes in which their intervention was not requested. It has been the policy of the chief mediator not to intervene without invitation unless the case was of unusual importance because of the number of persons involved in the strike or lockout, the inconvenience suffered by the public, or the outbreak of violence.

General Results of Mediation.—The Massachusetts board, the New York bureau, and the chief mediator and his assistants in Ohio have done work of great value in their respective States in preventing strikes and securing settlements of strikes or lockouts which have already occurred. Relative to

the total number of strikes and lockouts
in these States since the establishment of
mediation machinery, the number in which
settlements have been secured by the mediators does not loom up large; but if the
cases in which the intervention of the mediator or mediators has been followed by a settlement agreed to in a conference called by
the mediator, or agreed to by each party
separately with the mediator acting as an
intermediary, be considered absolutely, the
value of the results obtained by mediation in
preventing or shortening the term of strikes
and lockouts is apparent.

TYPES OF MEDIATORIAL SERVICE

The experience of the Massachusetts, New
York, and Ohio mediators makes it clear
that there is an opportunity for competent
mediators to render several distinct types of
service in bringing to an agreement parties

who have been unable to reach an agreement by themselves. These will be taken up. in order.

1. Many, if not most, strikes and lockouts occur before the matters in dispute have been thoroughly thrashed out and before either side has indicated the utmost that it is willing to concede to secure a settlement. It happens occasionally that the terms that each side is willing to accept if it can get no better terms are such as to make a settlement possible, yet there are obstacles to the frank negotiations which would make this clear. Obviously these obstacles are more likely to be present if the employer and the workmen have already broken off friendly relations. The strike or lockout usually throws the parties apart in irritation, if not in anger, and neither is in a mood for calm discussion or frank bargaining. One side or both may be unwilling to ask the other for a conference.

MEDIATION

In many cases the employer is irritated because a strike has been called without what he considers sufficient warning or discussion of the workmen's demands. In other cases the employer is unaccustomed to dealing with a union and is irritated because union officials not in his employ are asking to be dealt with as the representatives of his workers. Employers in this frame of mind will not go into conference with the workers' representatives at the request of the latter. On the other hand, the workers may be incensed at what they consider the too light treatment of their demands by the employer, or his failure to treat their representatives with proper consideration, and are determined to stand out until the employer accepts their demands or asks their representatives for a meeting for the discussion of their terms.

The service which the successful mediators have rendered in situations of this kind is that of getting before each party the fact that there are terms which both sides are really willing to accept as a settlement. The method which has been followed in most cases by the state mediators is that of bringing the parties together in a conference with the mediator and persuading them to discuss their differences calmly and frankly. If the terms each is willing to accept can be brought out in a conference of this kind the settlement by joint agreement will follow as a matter of course. The task of the mediator is to overcome the reluctance of one or both parties to meeting the other in conference and to keep them from still further irritating each other when they come together.

Most of the settlements secured by the state mediators have been secured through such joint conferences. If the parties can be induced to hold a conference of this kind and a settlement results, a long step has been taken toward collective bargaining for the future. The fact that they have met and discussed issues with each other directly and have arrived at an agreement on the points in dispute makes it much more likely that when differences arise later the parties will meet in joint conference on their own initiative and attempt to adjust their differences by negotiation.

A relatively large number of the settlements which have been secured by mediators through bringing the parties into conference have been in cases in which the strike or lockout was threatened or prolonged because of the refusal of the employer to confer with any representative of a union. It frequently happens that an employer refuses to meet a trade union official on the ground that he will deal only with his own employees, when, as a matter of fact, the higher trade union official is the one man on the workers' side who has the authority, grasp of the situation, and temperament to negotiate a satisfactory settlement. For example, the employer may refuse to "recognize the union" to the extent of dealing with a union officer, because he assumes that recognizing the union necessarily involves accepting the closed shop rule, although the union may be one that is willing to make an agreement without that rule. Under these circumstances, if the mediator can get the employer and the proper union officer together in a frank conference, the employer may have his fears removed and find that the union officer is willing to accept terms that the employer is willing to grant.

The mediator has frequently succeeded in getting the parties together, after one has definitely refused to confer with the other directly, by inviting both into conference with him at the same time and place. An employer who has refused to confer with a trade union officer will often come to a conference with the mediator even though he knows that one or more representatives of the union will be there, because he feels that he is going to a conference primarily with the mediator, and is not dealing with the union representatives as such. He goes as a matter of courtesy to the mediator. A conference of this kind may develop, and often has developed, into a direct conference between the interested parties and finally into a settlement.

Numerous instances of settlements secured in this way could be given. A good illustrative case is that of the settlement of a strike of the employees of a rope factory in Auburn, New York, in March, 1913. This case presented a familiar problem, that of the refusal of an employer to deal with the representatives of a newly formed union of his employees. The strike occurred because several employees who were officers of recently organized local unions of the United Textile Workers were discharged. After the strike had been inaugurated the strikers made wage demands and also demanded the recognition of their unions. The president of the United Textile Workers then went to Auburn to advise the strikers and otherwise aid in the conduct of the strike. When the state mediators arrived at Auburn they found that the officials of the company were unwilling to deal with either the officers of the local union or the president of the national union, and that the strikers were firm in their refusal to go back until they had received concessions as an organized body. The chief mediator, with the assistance of one of the directors of the company, finally prevailed on the president of the company to meet the president of the national union unofficially. This meeting led to a formal conference, in which the local union committee was included, and at this conference terms of settlement were agreed upon.

A similar example may be taken from the mediation activities of the Massachusetts board. A few years ago 350 glass cutters were locked out by an employer in New Bedford in anticipation of a wage demand, and the employer refused to meet the president of the American Flint Glass Workers' Union, who had taken charge of the dispute for the men. Fortunately for the settlement of that case the employers' representative on the board was a citizen of New Bedford and the president of the union appealed to him to use his good offices to bring about a conference. The member of the board secured a conference between the employer and the president of the union and an agreement was quickly reached.

After the parties have been brought into

joint conference it is difficult, sometimes, to keep them together. Before the parties can clear up matters sufficiently to see their way to an agreement, suspicions may arise on one side or both as to the real motives of the other in negotiating. In April, 1913, for example, the Massachusetts board learned that a strike of telephone operators in Boston was imminent. After interviewing the parties separately, the board was able to bring them together in a three-cornered conference. Such good progress was made in this conference that the board advised them to confer by themselves until all the differences on which they could reach agreement were disposed of, and to consider submitting to arbitration any points on which they found they could not agree. The parties agreed to do this and to reach a decision on the arbitration suggestion in two days.

But the following day, Tuesday, operators

began to arrive in Boston from other cities, to take the places of those operators who might go on strike. This threatened seriously to put an end to the negotiations, as the operators feared that the company was continuing the conferences merely to gain time to bring in strike-breakers. The board then got in touch with the parties again. The company explained that it was willing to continue negotiations in entire good faith, but it had to be prepared to continue its service in case no agreement could be reached and a strike should take place. Both parties then agreed to resume the conference the next day, Wednesday. At the request of the workers a committee from the Boston Chamber of Commerce met with the parties and also acted at times as a confidential go-between. The conferences lasted all through Wednesday and through Wednesday night until five o'clock Thursday morning, at which time a settlement was agreed to by the parties.

2. In a smaller number of cases the mediators have brought about a settlement by acting as confidential intermediaries between the parties. In these cases each party agrees conditionally to certain terms with the intermediary without knowing what the other party is willing to concede. It frequently happens that the parties, though willing to confer with each other, will not disclose to each other the most they will concede in order to get a settlement. Each may fear that if it offers a concession contingent upon the yielding of some particular thing by the other side, the latter will take this offer as a sign of weakness and refuse to concede as much as it otherwise would. Each side thus allows the conferences to end without stating its best terms, in the hope that the other will speedily offer better terms, when, as a mat-

ter of fact, the most one is willing to give and the least the other will take are really overlapping.

This is not likely to occur in a well developed system of collective bargaining. Where such systems have been long established, neither party will ordinarily allow the conferences to end in a disagreement without stating the limit it is willing to go at that time to reach a settlement. In other words, each side will offer as good terms to the other directly as it would be willing to offer confidentially to an intermediary. But where the joint conference method of collective bargaining is not well developed, deadlocks due merely to lack of frankness are likely to occur. This liability is especially great if the parties are looking forward to the possibility of arbitration in case no settlement is reached in conference. Each side is then fearful of offering a concession in conference which will be assumed as a starting point by the other if negotiations are broken off and later resumed or if the whole case is later submitted to arbitration.

In all cases of this kind the problem of the mediator is not to get the parties together in conference, but to secure from each side a confidential statement of the limits of its position. He has then merely to get each party to agree with the other to terms already agreed to conditionally with him. It is this confidential intermediary type of mediation which has proved so successful in federal mediation in interstate railway disputes under the Erdmann and Newlands acts. In intrastate disputes confidential intermediary action seems most likely to be successful in disputes involving recently organized workers. In such cases an employer will often accept mediation of this kind in preference to entering a joint or even a three-cornered conference, since it commits him to nothing. If the employees will not accept the terms which he is willing to grant, his own position is not weakened by the public offer of concessions.

The chief mediator of Ohio has found this confidential-intermediary type of mediation the more acceptable type. "Joint conferences," he states, "except in cases where the employees have been organized for a number of years and are accustomed to dealing with their employers through committees, are often productive of bitterness and for that reason are seldom held by the mediators." Apart from this, however, he favors the confidential type of mediation as a matter of policy because, as he puts it, "mediation under this plan does not disclose to either side either the weak points or the strong points in the position of the opposing side." [1]

---

[1] These statements are taken from a report pre-

MEDIATION AND ARBITRATION

Mediation of this intermediary type in strikes involving unorganized workers, even when it is successful, is naturally less likely to result in a direct agreement between the parties than when the terms of agreement are worked out in joint conference. The Ohio mediators have, however, brought about some direct agreements by intermediary mediation in strikes of this kind.

The Massachusetts mediators generally try to bring the parties together in conference as soon as possible, but at times find it necessary to secure conditional agreement to suggested terms of settlement from each party separately before bringing the parties together. For example, a textile strike of 700 operatives in two mills in Barre in March, 1912, was brought to an end in this way.

pared by the chief mediator, Mr. Fred C. Croxton, on " Mediation of Industrial Disputes in Ohio, January, 1914 to June, 1916," published in the *Bulletin of the Industrial Commission of Ohio,* Vol. III, No. 4.

MEDIATION

The hours of the women workers had to be reduced from fifty-six to fifty-four to conform with the new state law and the hours of all employees were similarly reduced. This raised the question of the rates of wages to be paid. The workers demanded an increase of fifteen per cent and the employers were willing to give but five. After five days there was considerable violence and arrests were made. Four days later the board was able to bring both sides to an agreement through separate negotiations with each. The next day both parties were brought into conference with the board and the agreement ratified.

3. In the above classes of cases the dispute was finally terminated by an agreement made between the parties. Each agreed to terms directly with the other after agreeing to them separately with the mediator. In addition there have been cases in all three

States in which the mediators have been able to secure a settlement by a separate agreement with each party when one party would not make an agreement with the other. The employer or employers may be determined not to make an agreement with the strikers as a body while on strike; the strikers, on the other hand, may be resolved not to return to work unless assured of certain concessions. In some of these cases the mediators have received guarantees from the employers that certain things would be done by the employers after the employees had returned to work, and have persuaded the men to return to work on their assurance that these concessions would be granted.

The New York mediators were able to settle two important strikes in this way in 1913. In January, 1913, 3,000 garment workers in Rochester went on strike. They presented no demands when they left the factories, other than to complain that the factories were doing work for houses in New York City whose employees were on strike. During the next two days many other garment workers joined the strikers and the employers announced on Saturday that if the strikers did not return on Monday their establishments would be closed. As the strikers did not return, the factories were closed. The number of those then idle reached 10,000. The state mediator came into the dispute a few days later and attempted to arrange a conference of the parties by personal interviews, but unsuccessfully. He then attempted, by writing to the parties, to get each to agree to a conference. The representatives of the workers signified their willingness to attend any conference he might be able to arrange, but the employers replied that each employer would meet a committee of his own employees. Separate meetings between employers and committees of their workers were then held, but these were fruitless.

The strike dragged along for nearly three weeks. The employers would not treat with the strike leaders nor agree to concede any increase in wages or reduction in hours to the strikers as such. They declared that they would take up any well founded grievance the strikers might have after they had returned to work, but were firmly resolved not to make terms with them as a body or to promise them anything while they remained on strike. Finally the strike leaders told the mediator that the strikers would probably return to work if they were assured that they would be given a fifty-two hour week, a re-reduction of two hours, and an increase in piece prices sufficient to keep their weekly wages the same, and that there would be no discrimination against members of the union.

MEDIATION

The mediator then made a public statement that he believed these terms would be granted if the strikers returned to work immediately. This did not constitute the definite assurance that the strikers insisted on and they refused to return. The Commissioner of Labor then ordered an investigation. Two other mediators came to Rochester to make up a board of investigation with the mediator already on the ground and the three mediators received a promise from the manufacturers that the conditions mentioned above would be put into effect in their factories immediately. The board then assured the strikers that these terms would be granted and faithfully carried out, whereupon the strikers voted to accept the terms and returned to work.

On May 1 of the same year, between 2,500 and 3,000 employees of fifteen department stores in Buffalo went out on strike. These employees had not previously been organized, and the strike was called under the guidance of local Socialist leaders, who, however, withdrew very early. When the state mediators intervened they found that some of the strikers had returned to work but a large number of clerks and drivers were still on strike and had been organized as local unions of the national unions in their respective occupations. The employers refused to confer with any representatives of the two local unions because the clerks and drivers had gone on strike without giving adequate time for negotiations and because of "the unreasonableness of their demands." The clerks and drivers refused to return to work unless concessions were made to them. After several days the mediators succeeded in getting promises from the employers that they would make certain changes in hours, wage rates, and other conditions of employment, if the strikers would return. These concessions were then made known by the mediators to mass meetings of the clerks and drivers, and the strikers voted to return to work.

4. The service of the mediators has not been confined to getting the parties to do what each was really willing to do and would have granted directly if it had been accustomed to dealing frankly with the other side. The mediators in all three States have secured settlements by persuading one side or both to concede something which would not otherwise have been granted. In fact, the most successful mediators in all three States have seldom given up a case in which their mediation was accepted, without as a last resort recommending terms to the parties. Sometimes concessions have been made in this manner because the side which was willing to concede preferred to accept the recommendation of the mediator rather than to

grant the same thing directly to the other party, but in many cases the recommendations have been accepted because the employer or the men did not wish to prolong a strike by the refusal of terms which an outsider of the experience, reputation, official position and personality of the mediator had decided would be a fair settlement.

In May, 1913, a threatened strike of machinists employed in a plant in Springfield was averted through the mediation of the Massachusetts board and the settlement was effected principally through the acceptance by the company of a suggestion made by the board. The company was a member of a national association of employers which is opposed to recognizing the machinists' union and it was alleged that a number of machinists had been discharged on account of their activity in the formation of a local union of machinists. An officer of the national union of machinists took up the case, but was unable to secure an interview with the employer. A strike was then decided upon.

At this point the board intervened. The employer informed the board that the manager of the labor bureau of the employers' association had full power to effect a settlement of the difficulty and that all negotiations must be with him. Upon interviewing the manager, the board found him willing to attend a conference with any representative of the workers whom the board wished to invite. A conference was then held, but no agreement was reached. The board then drew up a notice which it suggested that the employer should sign and post in his factory. This notice stated that there would be no discrimination against any workman "because of any affiliation," that the company would rectify discrimination when proved, and that the company would "receive a committee representing the employees of any one department for the purpose of a friendly discussion of any real or fancied grievance." After consideration this was agreed to by the employer. The cases of certain men who had been discharged were then taken up and disposed of and the proposed strike was called off.

5. Sometimes the mediator's recommendation is one that settles the particular dispute to the satisfaction of both parties, not merely a recommendation that one side grant something to the other that it is reluctant to concede. Neither party is asked to sacrifice the point it believes to be at stake; the apparently conflicting interests are harmonized. The opportunity to render this kind of service is naturally greatest in disputes between parties who have not been dealing with each other under a well developed system of col-

lective bargaining. The parties themselves are not able to find a solution of the difficulty, and there appears to be no settlement open which does not involve the giving up by one side of more than it is willing to give up without a fight. In such cases, the experienced mediator, through repeated handling of similar cases and an understanding of what each side is trying to secure, may be able to find a solution that safeguards the interests of both parties.

The Massachusetts board rendered this type of service in a discharge case in Boston, in February, 1913. An engineer had been discharged under circumstances that led the engineer and his union to contend that he had been dismissed unjustly. The employer refused to reinstate the man and a strike was threatened. The board suggested that the difficulty be met by the company's agreeing to reinstate the man on the understanding that he would immediately give notice of resignation. The employer was willing to reinstate him provided that he did not have to continue to employ him. The engineer, on the other hand, did not care to remain with that employer, though he was unwilling to accept the stigma of discharge. Thus both parties were satisfied with the terms of settlement.

Another example may be taken from the recent history of the Massachusetts board. A contracting company with headquarters in Boston was putting up a building in another Massachusetts city and had subcontracted the steam-fitting work. The Boston company had not stipulated that the subcontractor should employ only union men and the subcontractor had employed some non-unionists. A strike was called against the subcontractor, which soon included the employees of the company in other trades on that building and threatened to spread to its building work in other cities. The contracting company was quite willing that the subcontractor should employ union steam-fitters only, but under its contract it was unable to force him to discharge the non-union men, nor could it take away the work from him without rendering itself liable for damages for breach of contract. The board suggested that on promise from the company to require in all its later contracts with subcontractors that only union men should be employed, the company's work on that particular building should be allowed to go forward. This compromise was accepted by both sides.

6. Finally, the mediators should be able to suggest settlements which do not merely dispose of individual cases but permanently compose the hitherto apparently conflicting interests involved in an important issue.

MEDIATION AND ARBITRATION

This is the highest type of service which the mediator performs. There is much opposition to mediation on the ground that mediation means a mere compromise for the particular case, that it results merely in the patching up of one break without removing the difficulty which caused it and which will undoubtedly cause others like it. This view often leads one or both sides to prefer to fight the issue out in the hope of establishing completely their own positions and so disposing of that question for some time to come. The mediator is doing constructive service of the highest kind when he finds for the parties a way out which is not merely a compromise, but a real solution of the problem, one, for example, which safeguards the workman from industrial tyranny or preserves his vested interest in the trade and at the same time leaves the employer free to safeguard himself against incompetent workers and to improve in legitimate ways the processes of production.

The securing of settlements of this type has not been frequently achieved in the past by state mediators. The example of service of this kind which comes most readily to mind is the work of Mr. Louis D. Brandeis in settling the long strike in the cloak, suit and skirt industry in New York City in 1910. The issue on which the parties split and which stood apparently hopelessly in the way of a settlement was the insistence of the unions on the closed shop and of the employers on freedom to employ whom they chose. Mr. Brandeis brought them to agreement finally on the basis of the "preferential union shop."

The chance to render service of this kind will not often present itself in differences between parties who have been working together under well developed systems of collective bargaining. It may, however, occur even there from time to time. It is only rarely that the employers and the men in one trade are familiar with the devices used in other trades in handling the same troublesome questions, as, for example, that of discharges. A mediator who is thoroughly acquainted with the devices successfully employed in the various trades in handling the particular issue involved in a serious dispute, and who has faced the same problem repeatedly in other cases, should be of great assistance to parties who are seeking a real solution of their difficulty. The possibility of rendering this high type of constructive service is real, and it furnishes one of the best reasons for the State's attempting to put at the disposal of the industrial public the services of high-class experienced mediators.

LIMITATIONS OF MEDIATION

On the other hand, too much must not be expected of mediation. It cannot be expected that the mediators shall always prevent the occurrence of strikes or lockouts or that they shall bring all stoppages to a speedy termination. The experience of the mediators in the States studied indicates that there are several classes of disputes in which mediation is likely to be of little effect.

Successful mediation requires that the employer shall deal with the representatives of the workers in the presence of or through the mediator, and if an employer is resolved not to deal with his workers as a body, either directly or indirectly, he will not accept mediation. If the employer is a member of an association which will support him in his refusal to treat with his workmen as a body, the possibility of successful mediation is even smaller. In these cases there is no chance for successful mediation until the strike has lasted so long that the employer is driven to accept a settlement with the strikers as a

body. In such circumstances a settlement
frequently can be secured by mediation
earlier than it would be sought or accepted
by direct negotiation. But if the workmen
are unable to hold out so long there is little
chance that mediation will be effective.

It could hardly have been expected, for
example, that the mediation of the Massachusetts board would be successful at the
outbreak of the Lawrence textile strike in
1912. The representatives of the employers
on the ground were not accustomed to collective bargaining; they were not accustomed
to acting together; and they were unable or
unwilling to proceed on their own initiative,
without orders from those who controlled the
companies financially. Moreover, the real
strike leaders were officials of the Industrial
Workers of the World whom the employers'
agents looked upon as revolutionists and
were determined not to deal with or to recog-

nize in any way, directly or indirectly. The strike had to go on until the employers were willing to deal with the strikers as a body and the latter were willing to return on terms that the employers could afford to grant.

For much the same reasons, the New York bureau found it impossible to bring about a settlement of a lockout of steel workers in Syracuse, N. Y., in May, 1913. The employers closed the mill because a labor organization had been formed among the employees, and posted a notice announcing that the mill would remain closed until it could be run by men who would signify their loyalty to the company by sending in their signatures individually. The company also insisted that the men should give up their union membership before it would employ them. The men, on the other hand, refused to give up their union membership or to go back except in a body, though they did not insist on recognition of their union. Both sides understood the issue and neither would compromise. Therefore the bureau was unable to effect a settlement.

The chief mediator of Ohio recently encountered a similar situation. The Flint Glass Workers' Union, in an attempt to unionize a glass factory in Columbus, had declared a strike. The employer refused to recognize the national union, declaring that he would close the factory before he would settle with the union. The union, which has a national wage scale made in agreement with a national association of glass manufacturers, insisted that the only logical basis of settlement was the agreement of the manufacturer to pay the same wages and grant the same conditions as are agreed to by the association. Neither side was willing to compromise and the mediator could do nothing to bring about a settlement.

MEDIATION

In another class of cases mediation is not likely to be successful because there is little need for the kind of help that the mediator brings to the situation. In this class of cases the parties are accustomed to dealing with each other in joint conferences and the strike or lockout is resorted to only after a lengthy period of conferences. Each side knows the other's position, but is determined not to accept it, at least not without a fight. Either can secure a conference at any time after the strike or lockout has been inaugurated, if it has any further proposal to make, and so does not need the services of the mediator for that purpose. If both are thus determined to fight it out to a finish there is little chance for a mediator to avert or cut short the struggle unless he can find a solution acceptable to both parties, and for some issues that is extremely difficult. If he is unable to find such a solution, he cannot hope to do more than bring the two sides into conference when one is so crippled as to be ready to concede something but not willing to ask for terms, and thus secure a settlement slightly earlier than would have been possible without mediation.

CHARACTERISTICS OF A SUCCESSFUL SYSTEM

A plan embracing the constitution and powers of a state agency of mediation is here outlined with respect to the officers who should mediate, the considerations which should govern their appointment, and the degree of discretion which should be left them as to whether and when to offer their services.

The Officers.—Mediation should be intrusted to a person or set of persons entirely distinct from those who are designated to act as arbitrators or to conduct public investigations. The function of the mediator cannot be most successfully discharged when there is a possibility that the mediator may be forced later to pass judgment on the contentions of the parties.[1] The plan of having a chief mediator and assistants appears to be better than that of having a board of three colleagues of equal rank. The nature of the work of mediation is such that, other things being equal, better results can usually be secured through one man, availing himself, if necessary, of the assistance of another man or two other men, but following his own judgment and giving a unity to the suggestions and recommendations made to the parties.

Obviously, it is much easier to secure one man with the proper personal qualifications for the work of mediation than to secure three. Moreover, a greater continuity of policy is possible under the chief mediator plan, and reputation gained through past

---

[1] See pp. 78, 94–95.

services is more valuable when associated with the name of an individual than with that of a board or bureau. Finally, one man acting with individual responsibility in all cases will accumulate more valuable experience and a more intimate acquaintance with men, with the industries, and with the issues that arise, than he would if acting as a member of a board. These are the qualifications, other than personality, which make for success in mediation, and that plan should be adopted which aids most in the development of them.

Appointment of the Mediators.—It is hardly necessary to insist that the creation of an agency of mediation will not secure the desired results unless the mediators command the confidence of the employers and workers in their ability and impartiality. If this is to be gained everything which causes the industrial public to mistrust the purposes for which the mediation office is conducted or the motives which govern the selection of the mediators must be avoided. It is, therefore, very important that the offices of chief mediator and assistant mediator should be placed above the belief that these offices are being used as a reward for party services, expected or past, or disposed of so as to "strengthen" a particular political party in any way other than through the faithful and capable performance of their duties by the incumbents. One of the chief obstacles to the usefulness of state agencies of mediation and arbitration in the past has been the belief of a large number of persons, workmen as well as employers, to whom their services have been offered, that the positions of the members of the boards or bureaus were "party jobs" and that the members were trying to justify in some way the existence of their sinecures or attempting to secure a settlement which would redound to the advantage of their respective political parties. It is very difficult even for mediators of proved ability, fairness, and tact to realize the full possibilities of usefulness while the impression now prevailing in many quarters as to the grounds of their selection and the motives which guide them in their intervention remains. Furthermore, if any employer or group of workers refuses to allow the state mediator or mediators to intervene in a dispute, it should not be possible that a real or alleged disregard for the mediator or mediators as mere party spoilsmen should be accepted by any considerable body of citizens as a full or even partial defense of the refusal.

The chief mediator should not only be free from reasonable suspicion that he is a party spoilsman, but should also have the confidence of the employers and workers of the State as to his knowledge and fairness in dealing with industrial relations. The standing of the office can not be guaranteed in these respects by any mechanical plan of selection, but it seems wise to place the selection of the chief mediator in the hands of a board which deals with industrial relations and which represents within its membership the interests of the employers and the workers of the State as such, but is intended as a board to be partial to neither. The industrial commissions which have recently been created in several of the states are intended to be boards of this character and in a State in which such a board exists it should nominate the chief mediator. The selection of the chief mediator by a board of this kind would probably secure for this officer a better standing with the employers and employees of the State than direct appointment by the governor without such nomination. Once appointed, the chief mediator should be regarded as the head of an independent department of the State Government and not made responsible to any commission or other department. His term of office should be of sufficient length to give him independence.

New York has furnished an example, for a number of years, of a bureau of mediation working under unfavorable conditions surrounding the appointment of its members. Until the creation of the Industrial Commission in 1915, the chief mediator and his assistants were appointed by the Commissioner of Labor and for a number of years that office was held by men who had previously been trade union officers. The last Commissioner of Labor to serve was an ex-president of a national union. Moreover, the four assistant mediators, all of whom have been in office for several years, are men who have at one time or another been connected with labor organizations.

In many cases neither the previous union

affiliation of the assistant mediators nor the fact that the chief mediator held his office through appointment by an ex-president of a labor union made them any the less acceptable to the employers, but in many other cases it did. A number of employers stated in interviews that they assumed that the mediators merely aimed to secure from the employer the most favorable possible terms for the men. An employer who holds this opinion is not likely to give the mediator his full confidence or to accept his suggestions. On the other hand, many employers stated that they found the mediators very fair. For example, one of the mediators who was formerly an officer of a labor organization has acted a number of times as the third man in boot and shoe price arbitrations in Brooklyn. The first time he served at the request of the employers, with the acquiescence of the men, and since then he has been called on as a matter of course by both parties.

The point urged here is that previous trade union affiliation does not necessarily disqualify a man as mediator. Many former trade union leaders have made first-class mediators in those cases in which their services were accepted in good faith by both parties, and they have, in fact, made themselves acceptable to many employers. But in many cases the trade unionist is handicapped. It is easy to see that he would probably be much less acceptable to an employer or association of employers opposed to dealing with labor unions than a mediator who had no union affiliations. The same objection lies also against a mediator who has not been a unionist, if he holds office at the pleasure of a chief who has been a prominent union officer.

An illustration is found also in the history of the Ohio board. There was always one trade union member on the board and for many years a well-known ex-president of a national union served as the representative of the workers. This man was personally well qualified to act in most cases, but he found that his former trade union connection prejudiced many employers against him. Entirely aside from their belief that he must favor union recognition, they were reluctant to deal with him because they felt that in receiving him they would be recognizing trade unionism, inasmuch as he was admittedly the representative of organized labor on the board. Disputes involving the refusal of employers to recognize unions have not been unimportant in Ohio. In its 1912 report the board gave as one of the chief causes of strikes and lockouts "the refusal of certain employers to recognize labor unions or deal with the officers, committees, or other authorized representatives of their workmen in the adjustment of differences." As the ex-president of a national union was the only salaried member of the board and consequently the one who naturally first attempted to get in touch with the parties, the opposition of so many of the employers to receiving him in good faith made it much more difficult for the board to get good results.

Similarly, a man who had been a non-union employer or the representative of a non-union employer or of an "open shop" organization would be unacceptable to a union as a mediator. It would probably be even more fatal to choose such a man than to choose a trade unionist. The undesirability of choosing the chief mediator from the trade union ranks is emphasized at greater length merely because union men are actually chosen much more frequently as state mediators than are representatives of non-union or open shop employers.

MEDIATION

The chief mediator should be allowed to nominate his assistants, if assistants are needed. If, as is assumed, he has had no previous trade union affiliations, he will find it helpful to have one assistant who has been a member of a labor organization and has intimate knowledge of the viewpoint and policies of labor organizations. On the other hand, he should also have the opportunity of securing the assistance of a man who has been an employer, or a manager or superintendent, and has thus had experience in employing and dealing with men. Until such time as the chief mediator gains the full confidence of the parties to controversies he will find these men of great assistance in opening the way for the acceptance of his services. Even after the mediator has won the general confidence of the industrial public, cases will arise in which unduly suspicious or obstinate parties can more successfully be brought to deal with the other party by an official who it is thought understands their case. The assistant mediators can be used also to make the preliminary inquiries in disputes, and the less serious or less difficult of these they will probably be able to settle without calling in the chief mediator. This plan has been tried in Ohio by the chief mediator and works very well.

Powers of Mediation.—It is important that the mediators should be empowered to offer their services before a strike or lockout actually occurs, if in the judgment of the chief mediator a stoppage is imminent. Provision should be made that either party may request intervention before a strike or lockout. Both the Massachusetts and the New York laws put cases in which a strike or lockout "is seriously threatened" on an equality, in this respect, with those in which a strike or lockout has actually occurred.

The same is true of the old Ohio law, and under the present Ohio law the chief mediator in the exercise of his discretion has intervened in such cases. In all three States the mediators are unanimous in the opinion that many disputes which result in strikes or lockouts could be amicably adjusted if the mediators had knowledge of the trouble before the strike or lockout occurs. In all three States, also, the mediators follow their own judgment as to whether a strike or lockout is really seriously threatened when informed that such is the case. That discretion should be left them.

If mediation has not been requested by one or both of the parties, the mediators should be allowed to use their discretion as to whether mediation should be offered, and if so, at what time, even in cases in which strikes or lockouts have actually occurred. It is not desirable that mediation should be offered in all cases immediately upon the occurrence of the strike or lockout. A number of strikes can be and are settled by the parties involved after a few days' cessation of work, without any serious inconvenience to the public from the stoppage. It is not desirable that the state mediators should intervene in such cases. On the other hand, in another large class of cases attempted mediation is almost certain to be fruitless in the first week or ten days of the strike or lockout. Sometimes, when the strikers are but newly organized, the union leaders wish to keep them out for several days at least, in order to further the work of organization and to test their unionism under fire. In other cases, each side knows the other's position and each is determined not to yield while it sees a good chance for a complete victory. Unless a public utility is involved it would seem better to withhold the proffer of mediation until the parties are in a mood to coöperate in the attempt to secure an adjustment; nothing is to be gained for the principle of mediation by prematurely urging mediation upon parties who are determined not to settle at that time. It seems better, therefore, not to impose the obligation of immediate intervention in all cases coming to the knowledge of the mediators. The mediators should be required to offer their services as soon as may be practicable in all cases in which their intervention is requested by one or both parties; and empowered to intervene in other cases at the discretion of the chief mediator.

II

The treatment of public investigation and public recommendation as a means of terminating labor disputes in which mediation has failed must, as in the case of arbitration, be confined practically to Massachusetts and New York. The present Ohio law, adopted in 1913, makes no specific provision for investigation, and the powers conferred upon the Board of Arbitration and Conciliation by the old law, of making an inquiry and publishing a decision on the merits of every dispute which it was unable to bring to a conclusion, were practically not exercised by the board. The Massachusetts and New York laws have produced a number of public investigations and subsequent recommenda-

66

tions which have led to settlements, and these results indicate that much can be accomplished by investigation and recommendation if these are made by boards in which the parties and the public have confidence. The experience of New York and Massachusetts in this field under their existing laws, when compared with the results obtained in Canada under the Industrial Disputes Act and with the results obtained by private conciliation boards, leads to the conclusion that the work of investigation and, if necessary, recommendation can most successfully be performed by a special board created for that purpose in each case. A plan for the constitution of special boards along these lines is therefore suggested.

THE EXISTING LAW

The Massachusetts law imposes upon the State Board of Conciliation and Arbitration the obligation of investigation in every case in which the mediation of the board is not followed by a settlement, for the purpose of ascertaining the cause of the strike or lockout and of placing the responsibility or blame for its existence or continuance. Since 1914 the board has also been required by law to "make and publish a report finding such cause and assigning such responsibility of blame," "unless a settlement of the controversy is reached." Prior to 1914 the making and publication of a report stating the cause and assigning blame was optional with the board, though the board was under obligation to conduct an investigation in all such cases.

In New York a "board of mediation and arbitration" investigates in cases in which the mediators are unable to secure a settlement, if ordered to do so by the Industrial Commission.[1] For these investigations the board is made up of the chief mediator and two other officers of the department, designated by the commission; [1] as a matter of practice two of the assistant mediators are chosen for this duty. In both Massachusetts and New York the board, when conducting an investigation, has power to compel the appearance of witnesses, to require testimony under oath, etc.

RESULTS

In neither Massachusetts nor New York has the power of conducting public investigations been widely used. The great bulk of the cases in which mediation fails to secure a settlement have been allowed to pass without such formal investigation and report. This is because the mediators believe that in these cases no useful purpose would be served by a formal investigation. The members of

---

[1] Until May 22, 1915, by the Commissioner of Labor.

the board have been averse to holding up one side to public disapproval, particularly after the issue has been virtually decided. They have felt that unless an investigation would lead to an agreement it would be bad policy for a board primarily constituted for mediation to hold a public investigation which could serve only the purpose of finding one side or both blameworthy. The same considerations led the old Ohio board to refrain from using its powers of public investigation and recommendation. Therefore, until very recently the policy in both Massachusetts and New York has been to conduct no further investigation than that necessarily involved in mediation, save in very exceptional cases.

In the past few years the Massachusetts board has been much more active in holding formal investigations with public hearings, in cases in which mediation has failed. It was in line with this stiffening of policy that the law was changed in 1914 so as to make the publication of a report, as well as an investigation in such cases, compulsory. Even now, however, the board does not conduct public investigations and give its reports wide publicity in all cases in which mediation fails to result in a settlement. If the board's more or less informal investigation and direct suggestions to the parties result in a settlement no further publicity is given the findings as to cause or blame. For the past several years it has been the policy of the board to make a "recommendation" to the parties after the investigation as to what should be done to settle the dispute, although it is not required by the law to do so. To frame such constructive recommendations, rather than to assign blame, has usually been its purpose in conducting its investigations, and in most of these cases the recommenda-

71

tions of the board have been accepted by the parties as the basis of a settlement.

The value of a public investigation and the publication of its findings by the board in an important strike was illustrated in the Boston street car strike of 1912. This strike followed the discharge of a number of men apparently for joining a newly formed union or for aiding in its organization. The company replaced a large proportion of the men by strike-breakers and attempted to maintain its service. It took the ground that it had filled the places of the men who had left and was operating its cars satisfactorily and that there was no strike on its lines. It refused, therefore, to confer with representatives of the strikers. The board communicated with the parties several times, but the company refused to confer with the strikers. The workers were willing to arbitrate but the company was not. About three weeks after the strike was inaugurated the strikers requested the board to hold an investigation.

The board held a series of hearings and about six weeks after the strike began made a report. In its report the board stated that the men were justified in believing that many of the employees had been discharged for joining the union or for activity in its formation, and that "many of the company's cars are being operated by men whose conduct does not meet the approval of the traveling public." It added a recommendation that the parties attempt by conference to arrive at an amicable settlement. About a week later an agreement was reached by the company and the representatives of the union, in which it was provided that certain matters with reference to which the parties were unable to agree should be left to the board for final decision.

In 1913 the board in at least two cases sent

a recommendation to the strikers, after conducting an investigation, to call the strike off. In both cases the strikers were for the most part immigrants who did not speak English and had left their work without first formulating and presenting their grievances. In neither case did they have an organization before the strike, and both strikes were conducted by leaders who represented the Industrial Workers of the World. The employer refused in both cases to deal with the strike leaders. The board's recommendation was made in both cases in the form of a letter to the strikers. In one case the strikers returned to work at once; in the other the strike collapsed about a week after the board made its recommendation.

Where the issue is more specifically one of fact, an investigation is very likely to lead to a recommendation which both sides will accept. Two of the cases on which the board made specific reports in 1914 were disputes over discharges. In one case, involving milk-wagon drivers for a Boston company, the decision was adverse to the strikers. In the other, the board recommended that striking laundry workers in Brockton and their employer submit the discharges in controversy to arbitration. In both cases the recommendations were accepted. In wage disputes, too, an investigation is likely to lead to a settlement by bringing out how the wages paid compare with wages paid elsewhere for similar work or how wages have advanced as compared with the cost of living.

If made upon application from both parties, a report on the facts found, which does not deal with the cause of the strike nor attempt to place responsibility, may have practically the effect of an arbitration. In 1914, the board made a special report "in the matter of the joint application of" a company "and its Dye House Hands for an investigation and a report." This investigation covered wages, output of the workers, and conditions. The board employed experts nominated by the parties and "heard the parties by their duly authorized representatives" as it does in arbitration proceedings on similar issues in the boot and shoe industry. It did not recommend that any particular wages should be paid, but reported that it found the conditions and wages at least as good as those given by the company's competitors and that therefore it had not found that the company "pays a wage which is unfair to its employees as dye-house hands." Both parties accepted this finding as conclusive; in fact it was understood before the investigation that they would. The employer had stated that he would give as good conditions and wages as the board found in the shops of other employers. This

76

was, therefore, an arbitration in everything but name, although the employer objected to accepting "arbitration."

This case suggests the possibilities of a kind of informal arbitration in cases in which the issue can be decided by the determination of matters of fact which are in dispute. This procedure is possible while a strike continues, whereas under the law arbitration by the board is not. There is nothing in the Massachusetts law, however, specifically permitting the board to investigate and report except to ascertain the cause of a strike and assign responsibility or blame.

In New York, also, investigation has been resorted to more frequently in the past few years than in the earlier years. Commissioner Lynch stated in his first report in 1913 that it would be his policy to order investigations in those disputes in which there is a large public concern. In pursuance of this policy public investigations were held in the next two years in several strikes involving public utilities or affecting the main industry of a community. A lockout of employees for membership in a labor organization, also, was investigated. In most of the cases a settlement followed the investigation, but in at least two cases the employers rejected the recommendations of the board of investigation. In one of these the employers publicly attacked the recommendation as against the evidence, and declared that the board was prejudiced in favor of the men. The trade union affiliations of two of the three members of the board and the fact that the Commissioner of Labor who ordered the investigation was an ex-president of a national trade union were cited as indicating that the board was not impartial. In another case—the lockout in the Syracuse steel mill referred to above—the Commissioner of Labor ordered

78

an investigation after the mediators had failed to secure a settlement. The board of investigation recommended that the company reëmploy the members of the union without discrimination against them because of union membership, but the company ignored the recommendation.

It thus appears that the use of the power of investigation has hastened settlements in Massachusetts and—in a much smaller number of cases—in New York. This has come about in two ways. The investigation has settled disputed points of fact or has shown the two sides that they were nearer together than they thought, and has consequently led to an agreement through further mediation or through direct negotiation. In other cases, the investigation has led one or both sides, usually one side, to recede from a position which it did not care to maintain in the full light of publicity.

MEDIATION AND ARBITRATION

In some cases the threat of investigation has undoubtedly led employers to accept terms of settlement which they considered unfair, in order to avoid having business affairs not directly connected with labor matters given publicity. This danger should not exist nor should coercion of this character be exercised. The only pressure which can properly be exerted through investigation is that of public opinion concentrated upon a recommendation believed by the public to be a fair basis of settlement.

PLAN FOR BOARDS OF MEDIATION AND INVESTIGATION

The experience of Massachusetts and New York leads to the conclusion that it would be very useful to make provision in all industrial States for the appointment of a board to hold an investigation, report on the salient facts, and make recommendations in any case in which such an investigation seems likely to hasten a settlement. The occasion of the appointment of the board, and its constitution, plan of action, and powers will be discussed in order.

Occasion of Appointment.—The decision whether an investigation should be made after the failure of mediation ought to rest with the chief mediator. This officer, after his work in the case, is better qualified than anyone else to decide whether investigation and recommendation are likely to be helpful in restoring industrial peace. Moreover, the right to call for an investigation, if the parties are inclined to be unreasonable, will give him a stronger position as a mediator in cases in which a settlement is delayed through obstinacy rather than in defense of a principle.

Constitution of Board.—Such investigations should be intrusted to special boards of three persons. One member should be nominated by each party to the controversy, but should not himself be involved in it, and these two should select a third. If either side fails to select a representative, or the two fail to select a third within a specified time, the State Board of Arbitration should make the selection.

There are several reasons why investigations should be conducted by special boards and not by the state mediators or by the State Board of Arbitration. In the first place, if a public investigation results in a recommendation displeasing to one of the parties, the acceptability of the mediators or arbitrators in the discharge of their main functions may be seriously impaired. The function of the mediator is of primary importance and his reputation for fairness should not be put in jeopardy by requiring him to make decisions on disputes. The Board of Arbitration, as is explained in the next chapter, renders its service by passing on questions submitted to it voluntarily by both sides. Moreover, the mere fact that mediation may be followed by an investigation in which the mediator will appear in the rôle of an investigator would prevent the mediator from securing those confidential relations with the parties which are essential to the success of his work as mediator.

Secondly, a special board made up in this way has an important advantage in that it gives each side a direct representative on the board. Another opportunity is thereby presented for representatives of the two sides to agree on terms acceptable to their respective sides before the investigation is carried to the point of a recommendation. Practically, the appointment of the special board offers another chance for joint conferences between persons who are representatives of the sides

83

but not parties to the dispute. The experience of .trades governed by agreements which provide for the reference of disputes to joint committees made up of the same number of disinterested persons from each side shows that the possibilities of this method of reference in disposing of disputes are very great. Moreover, even if the two representatives cannot reach an agreement by themselves they may be brought into agreement by the chairman acting as a mediator. For this reason the board should be termed a board of "mediation and investigation," or of "conciliation and investigation" as in Canada. In the operation of the Canadian Industrial Disputes Act the chairman of the board has in many cases brought the other two members into an agreement on a recommendation. The success of the boards as agencies of conciliation is due largely to the fact that so many of the boards have had as chairmen persons who had previously acted in that capacity.

Publication of Recommendations.—If no agreement results during the investigation, the report of the board of mediation and investigation, including its recommendations, should be transmitted to the parties and made public. The parties should be invited to a conference with the board at which the recommendations are explained and the grounds on which they are based stated. If the parties accept the recommendations of the board, provision should be made for convening the board later if any dispute as to the meaning of the terms of the recommendations arises.

Powers of the Board.—The board of mediation and investigation should be given the same powers of investigation as are now conferred on boards of investigation in Massachusetts and New York. The expenses of the investigation, including a proper per diem allowance to the members of the board, should be paid by the State.

In certain classes of disputes, such as those affecting transportation agencies and other public utilities, the public is deeply concerned that there shall be no interruption of service. It is not proposed to prohibit strikes or lockouts in these cases but it is believed that the adoption of the plan here outlined would greatly minimize, if it did not entirely prevent such interruptions. Great pressure would rest upon both parties to refrain from hostilities until after the board of mediation and investigation had made its report, since any other course would bring public condemnation. The recommendations made by the board would also become a rallying point for public opinion, if the public had confidence in the board. Experience up to the present has not clearly established that legal prohibitions would be more effective in preventing interruptions of work. Both in Australasia and in Canada such interruptions have occurred in spite of laws prohibiting them.

In 1912, Sir George Askwith, Chairman of the Industrial Council of the United Kingdom, who has had an extensive experience in dealing with industrial disputes, made a study of the operation of the Canadian Industrial Disputes Act. In his report to the Imperial Government on the subject he expressed the following views as to the compulsory features of the act:

It will have been gathered from the preceding explanation of the working of the Act that where it was frankly accepted as a means of preventing disputes it has worked extremely well, but where, for reasons, some apparent and others which can only be guessed at, its introduction has been resented, it has not succeeded to the same extent. In such latter cases where, by the imposition of penalties, efforts have been made to enforce the

Act the results have not been satisfactory. . . .

The question then arises, what is the real value of the Act, and can any points in the Act be suitably adapted to this country? Is the restriction upon the right of proclaiming a lockout or strike so much of the essence of the Act as to make the Act of no effect if such restrictions were not compulsory? And do the penalties which are proposed to be enforced for breach of the restrictions of the Act add to its value?

In my opinion the real value of the Act does not lie in either of these propositions, and certainly not in the second. The pith of the Act lies in permitting the parties and the public to obtain full knowledge of the real cause of the dispute, and in causing suggestions to be made as impartially as possible on the basis of such knowledge for dealing with the existing difficulties, whether a strike or lockout has commenced or not. This action on behalf of the public allows an element of calm judgment to be introduced into the dispute which, at the time, the parties themselves may be unable to exercise.

III

ARBITRATION

Except in Massachusetts, but few disputes have been submitted to the state board for arbitration. In New York no case has been submitted to the arbitration of the state bureau in the past few years, and in Ohio the work of the state board was confined practically to mediation for years before its abolition in 1913. The present Ohio law makes no provision for a permanent state board of arbitration. This difference in the records of the boards in favor of the Massachusetts board is due in part to differences in the laws constituting the boards, but in larger part it is due to the activity of the board in making itself useful and so establishing a reputation for impartiality. An analysis of the results obtained in the three States leads to the conclusion that there are opportunities for a permanent board to render real service and that a board of the Massachusetts type would secure results worth while in the industrial States.

EXISTING LAW

The Arbitrators.—The Massachusetts and New York laws make provision for a state board of arbitration which is authorized to decide all disputes voluntarily submitted by both parties. Until 1913, provision was made in Ohio for such a board. In Massachusetts the board of arbitration is also the board of mediation. In New York the board is made up of the chief mediator and two other officers of the Department, designated by the Industrial Commission.[1]

Powers of the Boards.—In both Massachusetts and New York the law provides that

---

[1] Until May 22, 1915, by the Commissioner of Labor.

no case may be submitted to the state board of arbitration while one of the parties is maintaining a strike or lockout. It is a prerequisite that the employees shall be at work and remain at work during the arbitration proceedings. Both parties must agree, also, to abide by the decision of the board.

The Massachusetts law empowers the board, or any member of it, to summon witnesses, administer oaths, and take testimony. The New York law empowers the board to subpena witnesses and compel their attendance, take and hear testimony, and call for and examine the books, papers, and documents of any parties to the controversy. In Massachusetts the hearings may be private "if requested by the parties"—that is, no public notice is given of the time and place. It is the practice of the board not to give such notice unless it is requested to do so by one of the parties. In New York the period for which the board's decision is binding is not prescribed in the law; in Massachusetts the decision is binding for at least sixty days, and for at least six months if neither party gives sixty days' notice of intention not to be further bound by it.

RESULTS

In New York very few cases have been submitted for arbitration to a state board, and in the last few years none at all. In Ohio, too, in the last few years of the existence of the board, no cases were submitted to it for arbitration. The Massachusetts board, however, has acted in a large number of cases. In the boot and shoe industry the agreements between the Boot and Shoe Workers' Union and the employers specify that all questions of wages or conditions of labor upon which the parties cannot agree shall be submitted to the state board for decision. In 1913, for example, approximately eighty awards were made by the board in this industry. These cases constitute the great bulk of the arbitration work done by the board, but they do not exhaust it. Thus in 1913, the board arbitrated in seven cases in other industries than the boot and shoe.

Only three of the seven cases involved the terms of a new agreement. Of the other four, two were discharge cases; another involved the right of the employer, under an existing agreement, to employ a particular person; and the fourth, the proper classification, under the terms of an agreement, of workmen into wage groups. The year 1913 does not seem to have been an abnormal year in the quantity or distribution of the board's arbitration activities, except possibly in the rather high proportion of cases involving the terms of a new agreement. Only one of the three cases in this class was submitted after a strike as the result of the board's mediation.

The Massachusetts board exerts a constant pressure upon all the parties which it aids in reaching agreements to agree to arbitrate points that they may be unable to settle in the future. Largely on this account, many joint agreements made in Massachusetts now contain provisions binding the parties to refer questions in dispute to the state board of arbitration, in the event of failure to adjust in any other way or to agree upon other arbitrators. The policy of the Massachusetts board—and of the mediators in the other two States as well—has been, on the whole, to encourage the parties to submit their cases to arbitrators of their own choosing. It is only as a last resort that they urge the disputants to refer questions to the state board for decision.

ARBITRATION

The experience of the Massachusetts board in arbitration warrants the conclusion that there is a proper and very useful sphere of activity for a permanent state board of arbitration. A number of questions arise from time to time in almost all trades which do not require a detailed knowledge of the industry on the part of the arbitrating body, as for example, questions of discharge in alleged violation of a clause in an agreement covering discharges. The existence of a state board makes arbitration more likely in such cases than if a special board had to be erected to pass on the case. There are certain other controversies which both sides are willing to have decided by the application of standards which are matters of fact ascertainable upon investigation. For example, in many piece-price controversies both sides

95

are willing to have the questions decided on the basis of what competing manufacturers pay for the same operations under similar working conditions, but each is unwilling to accept the figures presented by the other side in support of its contention. It would be easier for the parties in such cases to submit the questions to an existing board which could appoint expert assistants to ascertain the prices and conditions in competing factories, than to establish a special tribunal to ascertain these facts. This is what the Massachusetts board does in the boot and shoe industry, and has done recently in at least one textile case.

There are other advantages to be derived from a permanent board. Members of a permanent board gain experience in handling cases and, if they do their work well, accumulate prestige for the board and accustom parties to the idea of arbitration.

ARBITRATION

Where a permanent state board that actually arbitrates from time to time exists, the framers of trade agreements are likely to agree upon the board as a court of last resort for the interpretation of the agreements. Finally, a permanent board which has among its members representatives of employers and employees and yet is, as a body, impartial can be utilized for the nomination of an odd member or odd members for special arbitration boards and for boards of mediation and investigation, when the other members of such boards fail to agree on a nomination.

PLAN FOR A BOARD OF ARBITRATION

The Arbitrators.—The experience of Massachusetts suggests that the plan followed in that State in the constitution of the arbitration board is a good one. One member should be an employer or a member of an employers' association, and one a member of a labor organization; these two should nominate the third, but if they are unable to agree he should be appointed by the governor without a nomination.

The members of the arbitration board should not serve as mediators. A mediator in a dispute can hardly escape receiving impressions as to what should be conceded by one or both sides. Moreover, strong mediators are likely to make suggestions or even recommendations as to what should be done. Having gone so far into the merits of the controversy they are, of course, not as acceptable to the parties as arbitrators as another set of men would be. Moreover, the usefulness of the mediators is likely to be greater if the idea that they may later have to decide the questions in controversy is not in the minds of the parties. A mediator's chief function is to help the parties to settle the dispute themselves, and this will appear more clearly, and make his services more acceptable at the outset, if there is no danger that he will urge that he and his colleagues be allowed to decide the terms of settlement.

The term of not more than one member of the board of arbitration should expire in any year. A six-year term is preferable to a three-year term. A comparison of the experience of Massachusetts with that of Ohio indicates that the annual salary method of payment is preferable to that of a per diem payment if men are expected to give the greater part of their time to the work. Both these boards, however, were also intended to mediate and to investigate as well as to arbitrate. It is doubtful if the work of a state board of arbitration—with no other function—would occupy the greater part of the time of its members, at least in the first few years. The case of Massachusetts is, of course, exceptional in that the arbitration agreements in the boot and shoe industry specify the state board of arbitration as the court of last resort. In other States it would probably be better at the outset to pay the members for the time actually given to the work. In appointing members to the board, care should be taken to select men who can serve whenever and as long as they may be needed. Men who are less well-known and esteemed will do more effective work—if honest, intelligent, and fair-minded—than men of known high abilities and of high reputation who would find it impossible to devote sufficient time and energy to the work.

Expert Assistants.—A feature of the Massachusetts law, which commends itself highly, is the provision made for the employment of expert assistants by the board in arbitration cases. Each party to the arbitration may nominate a person or persons to act as an expert assistant to the board and the board may then appoint one from the nominees of each side. The function of the expert assistants is to obtain for the board, under its direction, "information concerning the wages paid and the methods and grades of work prevailing in establishments within the commonwealth similar to that in which the controversy exists." The experts must be heard by the board before its final decision in the case is handed down. They are paid by the State at the rate of seven dollars a day and traveling expenses.

The employment of experts is confined almost exclusively to the cases submitted from the boot and shoe industry, because nearly all of the cases from that industry are piece-price cases, while very few of the cases from other industries are of this kind. The experts make their inquiries together and may not submit any evidence to the board on which they are not agreed. The success of the board as a board of arbitration for the boot and shoe industry is due chiefly to the use of the expert assistants. It seems advisable, therefore, that similar provision for the employment of expert assistants nominated by the parties should be made in any plan of state arbitration. The subject matter of their inquiries should not, however, be limited to wages paid and the methods and grades of work prevailing; the board should be allowed to direct them to inquire into and report on any matters which the board feels are pertinent to the case.

Powers of the Board.—The arbitration board should be given all the powers in the way of compelling the attendance of witnesses and testimony under oath, and the production of books and papers, which it requires to secure the information necessary to reach a decision. The need of compulsion

102

will seldom arise, however, for parties who submit voluntarily to arbitration will ordinarily supply the board with all the information in their possession. Yet the parties will be more likely to submit to arbitration such questions as piece prices, if assured that the board will be able to get exact data. Moreover, it may be desirable for the board to secure trustworthy information as to wages or working conditions in establishments not involved in the controversy, and such data may not be obtainable unless the board has the powers of a court. It should be stipulated that no information as to an employer's business except as to wages or working conditions shall be made public by the board unless he agrees beforehand that it shall be.

ENCOURAGEMENT OF FORMATION OF SPECIAL BOARDS

In all three of the States studied a preference was found, in most classes of cases, for special boards over a permanent state board, as an arbitrating body, and in all three States the laws encourage the formation of such boards. Both employers and workers expressed generally a disinclination to leave matters to the decision of persons who "know nothing about the business." In fact, the cases which are likely to be referred to a permanent State board in any number are limited in character—cases involving discharges in alleged violation of agreement, the interpretation of existing agreements, and the settlement of piece prices when both sides are satisfied to accept prices set on the basis of what competing factories are paying. In all these cases there is agreement between the parties as to the general principles which should govern the decision—it is merely the application of the principle which is in doubt. In such matters as the basic or minimum rate of wages to be paid, the length of the work-

ing day, and the ratio of apprentices, the
parties, if they are willing to arbitrate at all,
will in all likelihood continue to prefer special boards constituted by themselves. In
Massachusetts, preference is frequently
shown for a special board when certain classes
of questions are involved, because it is felt
that the state board will decide these questions by the application of certain standards
which the party is not willing to accept.
For example, it is widely believed that the
board will decide a wage demand by comparison with wages paid for the same work under
similar conditions elsewhere in the State.
Workers who are receiving higher wages
than are paid in competing cities will, therefore, naturally avoid arbitration by the state
board.

One of the clearest opportunities for service by the State in promoting resort to arbitration lies in facilitating the formation of

special boards of arbitration through aiding the appointees of the parties in the selection of the odd man or men. The state board of arbitration is the logical body to perform this duty for the State. The law should therefore specifically empower the state board, when requested, to select a man or men to act with the appointees of the parties. It should also allow the state board itself to act with the appointees if invited by them.

In all three of the States studied, as noted above, the law encourages the formation of special boards, known as "local" or "temporary" boards. The New York and Massachusetts laws prescribe the constitution of these boards. The New York law provides that one member must be chosen by the employer or employers and one by the employees and that these two shall select the third. The Massachusetts law provides that the local board shall be made up in the same way or composed of "three members mutually agreed upon."

The New York law allows the local board, through its chairman, to "subpena witnesses, compel their attendance, and to take and hear testimony." It does not give the local boards the power given to the state board to "call for and examine books, papers and documents of any parties to the controversy." Under the Massachusetts law and the old Ohio law local boards have all the powers of the state board, and as any member of the board in Massachusetts has all the powers of the board to summon and examine witnesses, books, papers, etc., it is understood by the state board that any member of a local board has these powers also. It has been urged that no member of a special board should be allowed to exercise these powers alone. The fact that the workmen's appointee on a local board has the power alone to compel the production of the employer's books, or to put the employer on the stand and question him, is said to deter many employers from submitting questions to such boards.

The New York law requires that for a local board to be constituted under the law with the powers described above, each member must sign an agreement to serve and must take an oath to discharge his duties faithfully and impartially. The Massachusetts law does not require that formal notice of the formation of the board shall be given. If each party selects its representative and these two select a third, they may proceed forthwith to exercise all the powers of the state board.

The New York law makes no provision for the payment of members of local boards of arbitration. The Massachusetts law provides for payment of the arbitrators by the local unit of government, but payment is to be made only with the approval in writing of the local authorities, and the remuneration is only three dollars a day for each day of actual service, which may not exceed ten days. The old Ohio law contained a similar provision. The local authorities in Ohio at times refused to pay, however, and the state board repeatedly urged that the law be so amended as to compel payment of the per diem and traveling expenses due, upon certification of the amount by the state board.

On the whole, these provisions seem to be of doubtful value in promoting resort to arbitration. If the State facilitates the formation of special boards by helping the parties to get a chairman it has done all that can reasonably be expected of it. The parties should themselves pay the members and defray the expenses of the proceedings. There seems to be no good reason for giving these special boards the powers of a state board in compelling testimony under oath or the production of books. If the issue hinges on a matter of fact which is ascertainable only by court procedure it should be submitted to the state board. If the issue is a matter of industrial policy the special board should contain within itself sufficient information as to the industry, or be able to get it, without using the powers of a court to decide the question before it.

IV

PROPOSED PLAN FOR A STATE SYSTEM OF MEDIATION, INVESTIGATION, AND ARBITRATION

The following plan contains the essential provisions necessary to give the foregoing suggestions legal effect.

I

There shall be a chief mediator, who shall be appointed by the governor on the nomination of the Industrial Commission for a term of seven years. He shall receive an annual salary of five thousand dollars and his necessary traveling expenses.

The chief mediator may appoint not more than two assistant mediators. Each shall perform such duties as are assigned to him by the chief mediator. The term of office of each assistant mediator shall be one year. Each shall receive an annual salary of not less than two thousand nor more than three thousand dollars, to be determined for each by the chief mediator, and his necessary traveling expenses.

Whenever a strike or lockout occurs within the State, or an industrial dispute arises which seriously threatens to terminate in a strike or lockout, the chief mediator shall, if requested by one or both of the parties to the dispute, endeavor to bring about a settlement of the controversy. Whenever the chief mediator has knowledge, otherwise than through a request for intervention from one or both of the parties to the dispute, that a strike or lockout or an industrial dispute which threatens to terminate in a strike or lockout exists within the State, he shall make inquiries as to the nature of the dispute and of the number of persons involved, and if in his judgment an offer of mediation is advisable he shall offer his services or those of one or more of the assistant mediators to the parties and endeavor to secure an amicable settlement of the controversy

II

If the chief mediator is unable to bring about an agreement in any industrial dispute or an agreement to arbitrate the dispute, and no settlement is otherwise reached, and if in his judgment it is advisable that a special board of mediation and investigation be appointed to endeavor to secure a settlement of the dispute, he shall make application in due form to the State Board of Arbitration for the appointment of such a board, and the State Board of Arbitration shall proceed forthwith to the establishment of such a board of mediation and investigation.

Every board of mediation and investigation shall consist of three persons, to be appointed by the State Board of Arbitration upon application made in due form by the chief mediator of the State.

Upon receipt of such application the State Board of Arbitration shall notify each party to the controversy that such a board is to be established and request each party to nominate in writing one person not a party to the controversy to serve as a member of such board. If such nomination is made within three days the State Board of Arbitration shall appoint the person so nominated a member of the board of mediation and investigation, and if either party fails to nominate a person within three days, the State Board of Arbitration shall appoint a properly qualified person to serve. The two persons so appointed shall nominate a person to serve as the third member of the board and the person so nominated shall be appointed a member of the board by the State Board of

Arbitration, and shall act as its chairman. If within three days after the appointment of the first two members no nomination of a third person is received, the State Board of Arbitration shall proceed to appoint a third member of the board of mediation and investigation and the person so appointed shall act as chairman of the board.

The chairman of the board of mediation and investigation shall convene the board as soon as may be practicable, in the locality in which the strike or lockout has occurred or is threatened, or if more than one locality within the State is affected, in that locality which in his judgment is most advisable, and the board shall proceed to ascertain the causes of the dispute and other facts pertinent to the failure of the parties to agree upon an amicable adjustment, and endeavor to secure an amicable settlement of the dispute.

MEDIATION AND ARBITRATION

If the board of mediation and investigation is unable to secure an amicable settlement of the controversy it shall make a written report stating the causes of the controversy and such other facts as in its judgment are responsible for the failure of the parties to agree upon a settlement, and shall recommend what should be done by each of the parties to the controversy. A copy of the report shall be transmitted to the governor of the State and a copy filed with the mayor or clerk of each city or town in which the controversy exists, to be open to public inspection. A copy of the report shall also be transmitted to each of the parties to the controversy.

The board may, if it deems advisable, appoint a time and place for a conference with each of the parties on the terms of its recommendations. Either party to the original controversy may at any time within one year from the date of the first report of the special board apply to the chairman of such board for a reconvening of the board to decide any dispute arising as to the meaning of any of the terms of the written recommendations made by the board, provided that such party has previously agreed in writing to be bound by such recommendation for a period of at least six months, and the chairman shall endeavor to reconvene the board forthwith for this purpose.

Before entering upon their duties the members of the board shall be sworn to the faithful performance thereof. The board shall be empowered to compel the appearance of witnesses and to administer oaths to witnesses and to compel the production of books and papers which it believes to contain information pertinent to the matters in dispute. The fees of witnesses for travel and attendance shall be the same as those for witnesses before the highest court of the State. The board may hold sessions in any locality within the State where it deems such sessions necessary. The board may also appoint properly qualified expert assistants, one upon nomination made by each party, to obtain and report to the board information necessary to the proper discharge of its duties by the board. The board may also appoint such other expert assistants as it may judge necessary. The expert assistants shall receive seven dollars a day for each day of actual service, and their necessary traveling expenses.

Each member of the special board of mediation and investigation shall receive ten dollars for each day of actual service, and his necessary traveling expenses.

III

There shall be a State Board of Arbitration, consisting of three persons, to be appointed by the Governor. Of the three members first appointed one shall be appointed for a term of six years, one for four years, and one for two years, and thereafter the term for each member shall be six years.

One member of the board shall be an employer, or shall be selected from an association representing employers of labor, one shall be selected from a labor organization, and the third shall be appointed upon the recommendation of the other two. If these two members fail to nominate a third at least thirty days prior to the expiration of a term or within thirty days after the occurrence of a vacancy, the Governor shall then appoint a third member without such nomination. The third member shall act as chairman of the board. Each member shall, before entering upon the duties of his office, be sworn to the faithful performance thereof. The board may appoint, and remove, a secretary, who shall not be a member of the board, and who shall receive an annual salary of not less than two thousand dollars nor more than three thousand dollars, as may be determined by the board.

Any industrial dispute existing within the State, which involves twenty-five or more persons and seriously threatens to result in a strike or lockout, may be submitted by the parties to the State Board of Arbitration for decision. The application shall be signed by the employer and by a majority of his employees in the department in which the controversy exists, and if signed by an agent claiming to represent a majority of the employees, the board shall satisfy itself that he is duly authorized to do so; but the names of the employees giving the authority shall be kept secret. The application shall contain a concise statement of the existing controversy and a promise not to resort to a strike or lockout pending the decision of the board, if given within two weeks of the date of the filing of the application, and to accept such decision as binding for a period of one year or until sixty days after written notice has been given to the other party, and to the board, of intention not to be bound by it.

Upon receipt of such application or applications signed by both parties to the controversy, the board shall proceed as soon as may be practicable to hear the parties or their duly authorized representatives and to take such other testimony, examine such books and papers, and institute such other inquiries as it may deem necessary for the proper discharge of its duties, and shall then make a written decision stating what shall be done or submitted to by each party to the controversy. A copy of the decision shall be transmitted to each of the parties and a copy entered in the records of the board. If either applicant fails to perform the promise made in the application the board shall proceed no further toward a decision unless requested in writing by the adverse party.

In all arbitration cases above described the board shall have power to summon witnesses, administer oaths and to compel the production of such books and papers as the board may believe to contain information bearing directly upon the matters in dispute. But no information as to the business of any employer other than as to wages or conditions of employment shall be received publicly or made public by the board without the consent of such employer. The fees of witnesses before the board, for attendance and travel, shall be the same as those of witnesses before the highest court of the State.

In all arbitration cases submitted to the board each party may nominate in writing fit persons to act as expert assistants to the board and the board may appoint one from among the persons so nominated by each party. Such expert assistants must be skilled in and conversant with the business or trade in which the controversy exists. They shall be sworn by the board to the faithful performance of their duties and shall, under the direction of the board, obtain and report such information as the board may judge necessary to the decision of the case, and they may submit to the board at any time before a final decision is given any facts, advice, arguments, or suggestions which they may consider applicable to the case. No decision shall be announced by the board in a case in which expert assistants have acted, without notice to them of a time and place for a conference with the board on the matters included in the proposed decision.

The board may appoint such additional expert assistants as it deems necessary, without nomination by the parties, which assistants shall be qualified in like manner and shall perform, under the direction of the board, duties similar to those performed by experts who are nominated by the parties. The expert assistants shall receive from the State seven dollars each for each day of actual service and their necessary traveling expenses.

It shall be the duty of the State Board of Arbitration to proceed immediately upon application in due form by the chief mediator of the State, to the establishment of a special board of mediation and investigation as provided in the act governing the establishment of such boards.

The members of the Board of Arbitration shall receive from the State ten dollars each for each day of actual service, and their necessary traveling expenses.

PLAN FOR A STATE SYSTEM

IV

Any parties to an industrial dispute existing within the State, who have agreed in writing to submit the matters in controversy to a board of arbitration to be made up of one or more persons chosen by each of the parties and one or more persons to be selected by the persons appointed by the parties, may, upon the failure of their appointees to agree upon an additional person, make a written application which shall be signed by both parties, or their duly authorized representatives, to the State Board of Arbitration, stating these facts and requesting the State Board of Arbitration to nominate a person or persons to act as an additional member or members of such board. Such application may also be made by the persons chosen by the parties to act as members of the board. The State Board of Arbitration shall within three days of the receipt of such application nominate a person to act as the additional member of the board. If requested by both parties the three members of the state board may act with the appointees of the parties as a board of arbitration, but when acting as members of such a board they shall exercise none of the powers of the State Board of Arbitration.

II

NATIONAL AGENCIES OF MEDI-
ATION, INVESTIGATION
AND ARBITRATION

V

PROPOSED NEW AGENCIES
THE NEED FOR NEW NATIONAL AGENCIES

The results achieved under the Erdmann
and Newlands acts naturally suggest that
provision should be made for national mediation and voluntary arbitration of the kind
provided for in the Newlands Act in fields to
which that act does not apply.   Under the
Newlands Act the mediators may offer their
services only in disputes involving railroad
employees actually engaged in train movement.   There are four large fields in which
national mediation and national provision
for arbitration seem desirable, to which the
Newlands Act does not extend: (1) disputes involving railroad employees not en-

gaged in moving trains; (2) disputes involving the employees of agencies of interstate commerce other than railroads; (3) disputes involving workmen and employers in two or more States; (4) disputes in which the intervention of the President of the United States has been requested in order to protect against domestic violence. The creation of a national agency of mediation and voluntary arbitration, with power to act in disputes in all four of these fields, would serve highly desirable ends.

At the present time mediation in disputes in all of these fields is possible through officers of the Department of Labor. The Act of March 4, 1913, creating the department, provided that:

The Secretary of Labor shall have power to act as mediator and to appoint commissioners of conciliation in labor disputes wherever, in his judgment, the interests of industrial peace may require it to be done.

130

PROPOSED NEW AGENCIES

The work of the department in this respect has been considerably handicapped by lack of funds to secure experienced mediators. There is reason to believe, however, that mediation in these fields would be much more effective if carried out along the lines of the Newlands Act than it can be made by the Department of Labor. The reasons for this will appear below. Moreover, it is desirable that certain provisions should be included, such as those for assistance in constituting boards of arbitration and for the formation of boards of mediation and investigation, which are not found in the present law and which are not likely to be most effective if their administration is vested in the Department of Labor.

If effective provision is to be made for mediation and arbitration in disputes of the kind indicated above, it must be national. It is evident, from an examination of the facts, that state agencies of mediation, arbitration, and investigation cannot be expected to meet the need. Even if effective state agencies were available in all the industrial States, as it is hoped that they soon will be, they could not be expected to secure settlements in disputes which are interstate in extent. State mediators are practically helpless, for example, in the face of a strike of railway shopmen which extends over the line of an interstate road, as such strikes tend more and more to do. The report of the State Board of Arbitration of Ohio for 1910 related a case in point. Trouble arose between the machinists and the Baltimore and Ohio Railroad Company at the Mt. Clare shops in Baltimore, over the attempt of the company to extend the piece-work system. Conferences were held between the national officers of the machinists' union and the general officers of the company, but they failed to result in a settlement, and after a referendum vote a general strike of machinists in the shops of the Baltimore and Ohio Railroad was inaugurated. The machinists at the shops in Newark, Ohio, were involved, among others, and the Ohio board found itself helpless to secure a settlement there. The board reported as follows:

The men at the Newark shop made no complaint as to wages, working conditions or other matters. They went out in obedience to the order of the union as they did at all other shops and were powerless to settle the matter. The strike involved twelve (12) shops and about nine hundred (900) men in Pennsylvania, Indiana, and West Virginia and six (6) shops and two hundred (200) men in Ohio. The strike was interstate in character and we were officially informed could only be settled by the general officers of the company and the national officers of the machinists' organization.

The same problem is presented in many labor disputes involving agencies of inter-

state commerce. A strike by organized
workers against such a company is likely to
extend beyond the limits of one State and to
involve issues which both sides wish to have
disposed of in a single settlement. This has
been the case, for example, in several strikes
on the Great Lakes. In at least one of these
cases the mediators of several States met
and acted jointly in offering mediation.
Their mediation, however, was unavailing.

There is another class of disputes, which,
though they do not involve interstate
agencies, resemble the class of disputes just
considered, in that they affect plants and
workers in more than one State and a settlement must be made for all at once. For example, the strike inaugurated in 1909 by the
Amalgamated Association of Iron, Steel and
Tin Workers and the Tin Plate Workers'
Protective Association against the American
Sheet and Tin Plate Company affected mills

in several States, and the attempts of state mediators to reach a settlement in the mills in their respective States were necessarily doomed to failure; the strike had to be settled as a whole. If any one of the large systems of national or district trade agreements should be interrupted by a strike affecting all the plants a similar case would be presented. If, for example, the Sanitary Potters' Association or the National Brotherhood of Operative Potters should resort to a lockout or strike against the other party at the expiration of an agreement, the mediators of one State—Ohio, for example—could not expect to secure settlements in the sanitary ware potteries in that State while the strike was still unsettled in New Jersey. In all likelihood no settlement would be reached for any until a settlement was made for all. The greater experience in dealing with disputes of more than local character that a national mediator would be expected to have, and the fact that he would be an officer of the United States and not merely an officer of a State, would give him a much better chance of bringing about a settlement than a state mediator would ordinarily have.

Within recent years, the President of the United States on several occasions has been called upon to protect the people of a State against domestic violence growing out of an industrial dispute. It appears clear that such disputes should be included within the scope of the activity of a national agency of mediation, arbitration, and investigation. At such times the state agencies are not in a position to exercise effectively their functions and if mediation or investigation is to be carried on it can only be carried on by a national agency.

The desirability of providing a national agency of mediation and of assistance in arbitration, to be available in the four classes of cases enumerated above, turns on the question as to whether the work of such an agency would be likely to be sufficiently effective to make its establishment worth while. The desirability of securing the settlement of such disputes by joint agreement or through submission to arbitration brought about through voluntary governmental mediation—if settlements can be secured in this way—is assumed to be beyond question. The experience under the Erdmann and Newlands acts, and that of state mediators in the three States in which the work of state agencies has been studied, indicates the strong probability that a national agency such as the one proposed could be of great service.

It is not to be expected, of course, that the great success of the federal mediators under the Erdmann and Newlands acts would be duplicated in the other fields which it is proposed to cover. The seriousness of the results which would follow immediately from the interruption of railway train service gives the mediators an assistance, in securing a settlement or inducing the parties to submit to arbitration, that would not ordinarily be present in these other cases, as, for example, that of a threatened or actual strike or lockout of railway shopmen. In this latter class of disputes there are, however, several distinct ways in which efficient mediators can aid in bringing about a settlement which will prevent a threatened strike or lockout, or in bringing an interruption of work to a close much earlier than would otherwise be the case. These types of possible mediatorial service have been described above in connection with state agencies of mediation and need not be further discussed here.[1]

Provision for national mediation in the

---

[1] See pages 9–46.

fields outlined above logically carries with it provision for the creation of special boards of arbitration in order to encourage the arbitration of disputes in these fields, which the parties are otherwise unable to settle. Experience under the Erdmann and Newlands acts has established the value of making in advance such facilitating arrangements for arbitration.

Finally, provision should be made for the formation of special boards of mediation and investigation in cases where mediation by the regular staff of mediators has failed to result in an agreement or in arbitration, and in which mediation by a special board is likely to promote a settlement, or in which a public investigation followed by a public report is deemed desirable. This conclusion is based on the results obtained through investigation and recommendation in Massachusetts and New York,[1] and, to a much greater extent, upon the results obtained under the Canadian Industrial Disputes Act.

PROPOSED AGENCIES OF MEDIATION, ARBITRATION, AND INVESTIGATION

The plans proposed for new federal agencies of mediation, arbitration, and investigation will be outlined in that order. The proposals include also the creation of an industrial council which it is believed will greatly further the work of mediation and will be of service also in the formation of boards of arbitration and boards of mediation and investigation. The composition and functions of the proposed council will be outlined in connection with the plan for a mediation commission.

THE MEDIATION COMMISSION

To carry out the work of national mediation, a mediation commission should be cre-

---

[1] See pages 65–76.

ated, consisting of three persons, to be appointed by the President. The duties now discharged by the board of mediation under the Newlands Act should be transferred to the commission. The commission should be empowered to appoint assistant mediators as occasion may require. It is desirable to have three members of full rank, not in order that they should act together as a board in disputes, but to make sure that a member of the board may be available to act promptly if two or three important disputes should arise simultaneously. Each of the mediators should therefore be a person of recognized impartiality in industrial issues and without affiliations which would make him unacceptable to either side in labor controversies.

It is hardly necessary to say that the office of mediator should in no way be regarded as a political office. To avoid even the appearance of party bias the term of office of the mediators should be long—at least six years—and the mediation commission should be distinct from any other department of government, as are the Interstate Commerce Commission and the Trade Commission. It is for this reason that the mediatory functions of the Department of Labor should be turned over to the mediation commission. The mediators should not be appointed by a cabinet officer, nor attached to any department under a political head.

The danger of having agencies of mediation administered by the party head of a department of government was clearly stated by the President of the Board of Trade in Great Britain in 1911:

One disadvantage of the existing system is undoubtedly that it brings into action and prominence the parliamentary head of the Board of Trade, who is necessarily a politician, though, in my opinion, none the worse for that, and a member of the Government, into disputes and conciliation which ought to be purely industrial. —If the action of the department in these matters could be still further removed from the sphere of politics or the suspicion of politics, it would give even greater confidence and there would be greater willingness by the parties to a dispute to seek the assistance of the Board of Trade.

There is an additional reason for not attaching the national mediation agency to the Department of Labor. It is generally understood that the Department of Labor is the department of government charged with studying the conditions and needs of the wage-earners and the best methods of legitimately advancing their interests. This makes employers generally feel that the officers of that department are more familiar with and naturally more sympathetic with the wage-earners' viewpoint than with that of the employer. It may be noted that when the legislation embodied in the Newlands Act was pending, both the representatives of the workers' organizations and the representatives of the railroad companies opposed the inclusion of the board of mediation within the Department of Labor.

The commission should be given considerable discretion in the determination of the salaries of the assistant mediators. It is highly desirable that the commission should be free to appoint assistant mediators who may have other occupations. The commission would thus be able to avail itself of the services of persons who have a knowledge of conditions and the confidence of employers and workers in particular localities or particular trades, but who would not be willing to give up their other occupations to accept permanent service with the commission.

The commission should be empowered to offer mediation in any case in which it is requested by one or both parties, or upon its own initiative in any case in which a strike or lockout has occurred or is seriously threatened. As has been noted in a preceding section,[1] there are several classes of disputes in which provision for a national agency of mediation appears to be of primary importance, and it is to be expected that in these classes of disputes the mediation commission will find its chief activity. It appears desirable, however, to leave the commission free to decide for itself in what disputes it will intervene.

It is important that the commission should be empowered to act before a strike or lockout has actually occurred. It is also very desirable that the commission be allowed to act without waiting for a request for its intervention. Experience under the Erdmann Act clearly established this fact and the Newlands Act removed the limitation upon the action of the mediators to cases in which the

---

[1] See pages 125–133.

intervention was requested by one or both of the parties. The experience of state mediators also leads to the conclusion that the mediators should be free to act on their own initiative.

The commission should also be empowered to organize a staff of trained investigators. These officers could be employed to make preliminary inquiries in cases in which strikes or lockouts have occurred or are threatened and in which the proffer of mediation is being considered, and to gather for the commission necessary information as to conditions in industries in which serious disturbances have occurred or are threatened.

The commission should also be empowered to organize a sufficient staff to gather and collate such information as to conditions of employment and industrial relations as it deems necessary to have for the proper performance of its functions. In order for the commission to be of the highest possible service, it is necessary that it should have at hand information as to the wages and conditions in the various industries and localities and the cost of living in different communities. Some of this information could be obtained from agencies already in existence, but more would have to be obtained through its own agents. In order to avoid duplication and to secure uniformity in methods of collecting and compiling statistics bearing upon these matters, the commission's staff should cooperate with the Bureau of Labor Statistics, other federal agencies, state labor bureaus, and other state agencies engaged in similar work.

The commission should also have on its staff persons who are familiar with the methods and devices employed in the various trades in which joint agreements have worked out successfully, as well as with the pitfalls which experience shows must be avoided. The commission would thus be in a position to advise employers and employees, state mediators, and other persons engaged in the promotion of the· amicable settlement of labor controversies.

Industrial Council.—As a part of the plan, it would be desirable to establish an industrial council to consist of an equal number of representatives of employers' associations and labor organizations. The President should designate at least ten leading employers' associations and ten leading organizations of employees, each of which should elect a member of the council. The duties of the council would be to advise the mediation commission and to advise the President and Congress on matters affecting mediation, arbitration, investigation and industrial relations generally. The council should prepare a panel of arbitrators from which the mediation commission should choose the members of boards of arbitration in cases in which the members of such boards selected by the parties fail to agree on the two other members. It should in similar manner select a panel from which the mediation commission should select the members of boards of mediation and investigation in case the parties to the disputes do not name members or the members so named do not agree upon a chairman. The council should be convened at least once a year by the chairman of the mediation commission, but it should have an organization independent of the commission and elect its own chairman and secretary.

Boards of Arbitration—In the event that the parties to an industrial dispute agree to submit a dispute to arbitration, application may be made to the mediation commission for the formation of an arbitration board.

149

MEDIATION AND ARBITRATION

The arbitration provisions in the plan here proposed are the same as those of the Newlands Act,[1] except that if the members of the board appointed by the parties fail to agree on the additional member or members, these shall be appointed by the mediation commission from a list prepared by the industrial council. It is desirable to keep the mediation commission as free as possible from any connection with any board which passes public judgment on the merits of a dispute. This is advisable in order to avoid anything which may make either party to a controversy feel that the mediators favor the other side, and also to secure for the mediators full frankness from both parties as to the terms they will accept, when the mediators are endeavoring to settle a dispute by acting as intermediaries. The further the commission is

---

[1] The arbitration provisions of the Newlands Act are given in Appendix I.

removed from the arbitration to which the parties are to be urged to submit if they cannot be brought to an agreement, the more frank the parties will be, in all likelihood, and the greater will be the chances of submission to arbitration if no other solution is found.   Under the plan proposed the only connection of the mediation commission with the boards of arbitration will be the selection of the members necessary to fill out the board from a panel agreed upon in advance by the industrial council.

Boards of Mediation and Investigation.— Provision should be made for the appointment of a board of mediation and investigation in any dispute involving interstate commerce in which the mediation commission fails to bring about a settlement or an agreement to submit to arbitration, and in which the commission judges that the appointment of such a board would be expedient.   Such a board should also be formed in those cases in which an industrial dispute has led to domestic violence and to an application to the President of the United States for protection, provided the President of the United States directs the mediation commission to form such a board.

These boards should be made up of one member appointed by each party to the dispute and a third selected by these two. The persons nominated by the parties should be familiar with the business and the issues in dispute, but should not be parties to the controversy. If either side fails to nominate a member within a specified time, or the two fail to agree on a third, the mediation commission should select the member or members.

The function of the board is to inquire into the nature and causes of the dispute and endeavor to bring the parties to a settlement or to an agreement to submit to arbitration. If the board fails in this, it is to make a public statement of the salient facts and a recommendation of the terms which should be accepted as a settlement of the dispute.

The boards of mediation and investigation should have power to compel the attendance of witnesses and their testimony under oath and the production of books and papers which it believes to contain information pertinent to the controversy under investigation. It should have power to conduct investigations outside its own sittings, through expert investigators. It is not proposed, however, to give the board power to enforce its recommendation or to prohibit the parties' resorting to a strike or lockout either before or after its investigation and recommendations.

VI

PROPOSED PLAN OF A NATIONAL SYSTEM OF MEDIATION, INVESTIGATION, AND ARBITRATION

ORGANIZATION

1. *Mediation Commission.*—A mediation commission shall be created, consisting of three members appointed by the President with the advice and consent of the Senate. The members shall be impartial in their relations to capital and labor. The members shall serve for terms of six years.

2. *Industrial Council.*—The President of the United States shall designate at least ten leading organizations of employers and ten leading organizations of employees to appoint representatives to act as an advisory body to the President, to Congress, and to

154

the mediation commission. This body shall be known as the Industrial Council. It shall give advice regarding the duties of the commission, the administration of its affairs, the selection of mediators, and shall make recommendations regarding legislation. The council shall also prepare lists of persons who may be called upon to serve on boards of arbitration and on boards of mediation and investigation. The council shall be called together at least once a year by the chairman of the mediation commission; it shall have an organization independent of the commission and elect its own chairman and secretary. The commission may appoint the members of the council to assist in its work in the same way as it appoints its subordinate officers. The members of the council shall be paid traveling and other necessary expenses and such compensation as may be determined upon. Provision shall be made for the removal of members by the organization which they represent.

3. *Subordinate Officers and Assistants.*— The commission shall have power to appoint, remove at pleasure, and fix the compensation of a secretary (and a limited number of clerks). The appointment of other officers and assistants, such as mediators, examiners, investigators, technical assessors, experts, disbursing officer, clerks, and other employees, shall be subject to the Civil Service rules. The commission shall select a committee from its own membership which the Civil Service Commission shall include in the Board of Examiners for conducting examinations and preparing lists of eligibles for such subordinate officers and employees as are required to have special knowledge or training. Such examinations shall include a thorough investigation of the education, training, and experience of the applicants, their success in handling men, and their ability in executive affairs, in order to determine their relative capacity and fitness for the office or position to which they seek to be appointed. If so required, applicants shall appear before the Board of Examiners for an oral examination. Additional rules and regulations concerning such examinations may be made by joint action of the Civil Service Commission and the committee of the Mediation Commission. Employees of the commission who are to act as mediators shall be permitted to accept appointments as officers of state or local governments if the duties thereof do not interfere with their duties to the commission. The commission shall be authorized to appoint, without regard to Civil Service rules, officers of state or local governments to represent the commission. An employee of the commission shall be permitted to continue with his private business if the duties thereof are not inconsistent with his duties to the council.

POWERS, DUTIES, AND JURISDICTION

4. *In Interstate Commerce.*—a. Mediation. Whenever a controversy concerning conditions of employment arises between employer and employees engaged in interstate commerce, either party may apply to the chairman of the Mediation Commission for its services in the bringing about of an amicable adjustment of the controversy. Or the chairman of the commission shall be authorized to offer, on his own initiative, the services of the commission. If efforts to bring about an amicable adjustment through mediation should be unsuccessful, the commission shall at once, if possible, induce the parties to submit their differences to arbitration.

b. Arbitration. Procedure shall be similar to that outlined in the Newlands Act.[1]

If it is necessary for the mediation commission to appoint arbitrators, they shall be taken from a list prepared by the industrial council.

c. Boards of mediation and investigation. If the parties to the controversy cannot be induced to arbitrate, and if the controversy should threaten to interrupt the business of employers and employees to the detriment of the public interest, the commission shall be authorized to provide, at its discretion, for the creation of a board of mediation and investigation consisting of three members. Of the three members of the board, one shall be selected by the employers, one by the employees, and a third on the recommendation of the members so chosen. The members selected by the employers and employees shall not have any direct financial interest in the dispute. If either

---

[1] This act is given in Appendix I.

159

side fails to recommend a member, he shall be appointed by the commission. If after a stated time the third member is not recommended, the commission shall select him. Appointments to boards of mediation and investigation shall be made by the commission from a list prepared for this purpose by the industrial council. The board of mediation and investigation shall offer its friendly offices in bringing about a settlement of the dispute through mediation. If mediation should not be successful and if the parties to the controversy refuse to arbitrate, this board shall have power to make an investigation of the controversy, and shall be required to submit to the commission a full report thereon, including recommendations for its settlement. This report and recommendation shall be given adequate publicity.

d. Compulsory Powers. A board of mediation and investigation shall have power

to administer oaths, to subpena and compel
the attendance of witnesses and the production of books, papers, documents, etc., to conduct hearings and investigations, and to exercise such other powers as may be necessary.
They shall not have power to prohibit, or to
impose penalties for, strikes or lockouts.

5. *Not in Interstate Commerce.*—It shall
be provided that the commission, or a board
of mediation and investigation created by it
may exercise the foregoing powers, except
the compulsory powers under Subdivision d
of Proposal 4, for settling industrial controversies between parties not engaged in interstate commerce.

6. *On Request of the State in which the
Controversy Exists.*—A board of mediation
and investigation may exercise all the foregoing powers for settling industrial controversies within any State, if the legislature or
the executive of the State has requested pro-

tection against domestic violence and the formation of such a board by the mediation commission has been directed by the President of the United States.

COÖPERATION

7. *Coöperation with State and Local Authorities.*—The commission shall be authorized and directed to coöperate with state, local, and territorial authorities and similar departments of foreign countries which deal with the adjustment of industrial disputes.

8. *Coöperation with Other Federal Agencies.*—The commission, as far as practicable, shall coördinate its activities with and coöperate with other Federal departments in the performance of their duties. The Secretary of Labor and Secretary of Commerce should be ex-officio advisors to the commission.

III

APPENDICES

APPENDIX I

THE NEWLANDS ACT

An Act Providing for mediation, conciliation, and arbitration in controversies between certain employers and their employees.

Be it enacted by the Senate and House of Representatives of the United States of America in Congress assembled, That the provisions of this Act shall apply to any common carrier or carriers and their officers, agents, and employees, except masters of vessels and seamen, as defined in section forty-six hundred and twelve, Revised Statutes of the United States, engaged in the transportation of passengers or property wholly by railroad, or partly by railroad and partly by water, for a continuous carriage or shipment from one State or Territory of the United States or the District of Columbia to any other State or Territory of the United States or the District of Columbia, or from any place in the United States to an adjacent foreign country, or from any place in the United States through a foreign country to any other place in the United States.

APPENDIX I

The term "railroad" as used in this Act shall include all bridges and ferries used or operated in connection with any railroad, and also all the road in use by any corporation operating a railroad, whether owned or operated under a contract, agreement, or lease; and the term "transportation" shall include all instrumentalities of shipment or carriage.

The term "employees" as used in this Act shall include all persons actually engaged in any capacity in train operation or train service of any description, and notwithstanding that the cars upon or in which they are employed may be held and operated by the carrier under lease or other contract: *Provided, however,* That this Act shall not be held to apply to employees of street railroads and shall apply only to employees engaged in railroad train service. In every such case the carrier shall be responsible for the acts and defaults of such employees in the same manner and to the same extent as if said cars were owned by it and said employees directly employed by it, and any provisions to the contrary of any such lease or other contract shall be binding only as between the parties thereto and shall not affect the obligations of said carrier either to the public or to the private parties concerned.

APPENDIX I

A common carrier subject to the provisions of this Act is hereinafter referred to as an "employer," and the employees of one or more of such carriers are hereinafter referred to as "employees."

Sec. 2. That whenever a controversy concerning wages, hours of labor, or conditions of employment shall arise between an employer or employers and employees subject to this Act interrupting or threatening to interrupt the business of said employer or employers to the serious detriment of the public interest, either party to such controversy may apply to the Board of Mediation and Conciliation created by this Act and invoke its services for the purpose of bringing about an amicable adjustment of the controversy; and upon the request of either party the said board shall with all practicable expedition put itself in communication with the parties to such controversy and shall use its best efforts, by mediation and conciliation, to bring them to an agreement; and if such efforts to bring about an amicable adjustment through mediation and conciliation shall be unsuccessful, the said board shall at once endeavor to induce the parties to submit their controversy to arbitration in accordance with the provisions of this Act.

APPENDIX I

In any case in which an interruption of traffic is imminent and fraught with serious detriment to the public interest, the Board of Mediation and Conciliation may, if in its judgment such action seem desirable, proffer its services to the respective parties to the controversy.

In any case in which a controversy arises over the meaning or the application of any agreement reached through mediation under the provisions of this Act either party to the said agreement may apply to the Board of Mediation and Conciliation for an expression of opinion from such board as to the meaning or application of such agreement and the said board shall upon receipt of such request give its opinion as soon as may be practicable.

SEC. 3. That whenever a controversy shall arise between an employer or employers and employees subject to this Act, which can not be settled through mediation and conciliation in the manner provided in the preceding section, such controversy may be submitted to the arbitration of a board of six, or, if the parties to the controversy prefer so to stipulate, to a board of three persons, which board shall be chosen in the following manner: In the case of a board of three, the employer or employers and the employees, parties respectively to the agreement to arbitrate, shall each name one arbitrator; and the two arbitrators thus chosen shall select the third arbitrator; but in the event of their failure to name the third arbitrator within five days after their first meeting, such third arbitrator shall be named by the Board of Mediation and Conciliation. In the case of a board of six, the employer or employers and the employees, parties respectively to the agreement to arbitrate, shall each name two arbitrators, and the four arbitrators thus chosen shall, by a majority vote, select the remaining two arbitrators; but in the event of their failure to name the two arbitrators within fifteen days after their first meeting the said two arbitrators, or as many of them as have not been named, shall be named by the Board of Mediation and Conciliation.

In the event that the employees engaged in any given controversy are not members of a labor organization, such employees may select a committee which shall have the right to name the arbitrator, or the arbitrators, who are to be named by the employees as provided above in this section.

SEC. 4. That the agreement to arbitrate—

First. Shall be in writing;

Second. Shall stipulate that the arbitration is had under the provisions of this Act;

Third. Shall state whether the board of arbitration is to consist of three or six members;

Fourth. Shall be signed by duly accredited representatives of the employer or employers and of the employees;

Fifth. Shall state specifically the questions to be submitted to the said board for decision;

Sixth. Shall stipulate that a majority of said board shall be competent to make a valid and binding award;

Seventh. Shall fix a period from the date of the appointment of the arbitrator or arbitrators necessary to complete the board, as provided for in the agreement, within which the said board shall commence its hearings;

Eighth. Shall fix a period from the beginning of the hearings within which the said board shall make and file its award: *Provided*, That this period shall be thirty days unless a different period be agreed to;

Ninth. Shall provide for the date from which the award shall become effective and shall fix the period during which the said award shall continue in force;

Tenth. Shall provide that the respective parties to the award will each faithfully execute the same;

APPENDIX I

Eleventh. Shall provide that the award and the papers and proceedings, including the testimony relating thereto, certified under the hands of the arbitrators, and which shall have the force and effect of a bill of exceptions, shall be filed in the clerk's office of the district court of the United States for the district wherein the controversy arises or the arbitration is entered into, and shall be final and conclusive upon the parties to the agreement unless set aside for error of law apparent on the record;

Twelfth. May also provide that any difference arising as to the meaning or the application of the provisions of an award made by a board of arbitration shall be referred back to the same board or to a subcommittee of such board for a ruling, which ruling shall have the same force and effect as the original award; and if any member of the original board is unable or unwilling to serve another arbitrator shall be named in the same manner as such original member was named.

SEC. 5. That for the purposes of this Act the arbitrators herein provided for, or either of them, shall have power to administer oaths and affirmations, sign subpenas, require the attendance and testimony of witnesses, and the production of such books, papers, contracts, agreements, and documents material to a just determination of the matters under investigation as may be ordered by the court; and may invoke the aid of the United States courts to compel witnesses to attend and testify and to produce such books, papers, contracts, agreements, and documents to the same extent and under the same conditions and penalties as is provided for in the Act to regulate commerce, approved February fourth, eighteen hundred and eighty-seven, and the amendments thereto.

SEC. 6. That every agreement of arbitration under this Act shall be acknowledged by the parties thereto before a notary public or a clerk of the district or the circuit court of appeals of the United States, or before a member of the Board of Mediation and Conciliation, the members of which are hereby authorized to take such acknowledgments; and when so acknowledged shall be delivered to a member of said board or transmitted to said board to be filed in its office.

When such agreement of arbitration has been filed with the said board, or one of its members, and when the said board, or a member thereof, has been furnished the names of the arbitrators chosen by the respective parties to the controversy, the board, or a member thereof, shall cause a notice in writing to be served upon the said arbitrators, notifying them of their appointment, requesting them to meet promptly to name the remaining arbitrator or arbitrators necessary to complete the board, and advising them of the period within which, as provided in the agreement of arbitration, they are empowered to name such arbitrator or arbitrators.

When the arbitrators selected by the respective parties have agreed upon the remaining arbitrator or arbitrators, they shall notify the Board of Mediation and Conciliation; and in the event of their failure to agree upon any or upon all of the necessary arbitrators within the period fixed by this Act they shall, at the expiration of such period, notify the Board of Mediation and Conciliation of the arbitrators selected, if any, or of their failure to make or to complete such selection.

If the parties to an arbitration desire the reconvening of a board to pass upon any controversy arising over the meaning or application of an award, they shall jointly so notify the Board of Mediation and Conciliation, and shall state in such written notice the question or questions to be submitted to such reconvened board. The Board of Mediation and Conciliation shall thereupon promptly communicate with the members of the board of arbitration or a subcommittee of such

APPENDIX I

board appointed for such purpose pursuant to the provisions of the agreement of arbitration, and arrange for the reconvening of said board or subcommittee, and shall notify the respective parties to the controversy of the time and place at which the board will meet for hearings upon the matters in controversy to be submitted to it.

SEC. 7. That the board of arbitration shall organize and select its own chairman and make all necessary rules for conducting its hearings; but in its award or awards the said board shall confine itself to findings or recommendations as to the questions specifically submitted to it or matters directly bearing thereon. All testimony before said board shall be given under oath or affirmation, and any member of the board of arbitration shall have the power to administer oaths or affirmations. It may employ such assistants as may be necessary in carrying on its work. It shall, whenever practicable, be supplied with suitable quarters in any Federal building located at its place of meeting or at any place where the board may adjourn for its deliberations. The board of arbitration shall furnish a certified copy of its awards to the respective parties to the controversy, and shall transmit the original, together with the papers and proceedings and a transcript of

APPENDIX I

the testimony taken at the hearings, certified under the hands of the arbitrators, to the clerk of the district court of the United States for the district wherein the controversy arose or the arbitration is entered into, to be filed in said clerk's office as provided in paragraph eleven of section four of this Act. And said board shall also furnish a certified copy of its award, and the papers and proceedings, including the testimony relating thereto, to the Board of Mediation and Conciliation, to be filed in its office.

The United States Commerce Court, the Inter-State Commerce Commission, and the Bureau of Labor Statistics are hereby authorized to turn over to the Board of Mediation and Conciliation upon its request any papers and documents heretofore filed with them and bearing upon mediation or arbitration proceedings held under the provisions of the Act approved June first, eighteen hundred and ninety-eight, providing for mediation and arbitration.

SEC. 8. That the award, being filed in the clerk's office of a district court of the United States as hereinbefore provided, shall go into practical operation, and judgment shall be entered thereon accordingly at the expiration of ten days from such filing, unless within such ten days either party shall file exceptions thereto for matter of law apparent upon the record, in which case said award shall go into practical operation, and judgment be entered accordingly, when such exceptions shall have been finally disposed of either by said district court or on appeal therefrom.

At the expiration of ten days from the decision of the district court upon exceptions taken to said award as aforesaid judgment shall be entered in accordance with said decision, unless during said ten days either party shall appeal therefrom to the circuit court of appeals. In such case only such portion of the record shall be transmitted to the appellate court as is necessary to the proper understanding and consideration of the questions of law presented by said exceptions and to be decided.

The determination of said circuit court of appeals upon said questions shall be final, and, being certified by the clerk thereof to said district court, judgment pursuant thereto shall thereupon be entered by said district court.

If exceptions to an award are finally sustained, judgment shall be entered setting aside the award in whole or in part; but in such case the parties may agree upon a judgment to be entered disposing of the subject matter of the controversy, which judgment when entered shall have the same force and effect as judgment entered upon an award.

Nothing in this Act contained shall be construed to require an employee to render personal service without his consent, and no injunction or other legal process shall be issued which shall compel the performance by any employee against his will of a contract for personal labor or service.

SEC. 9. That whenever receivers appointed by a Federal court are in the possession and control of the business of employers covered by this Act the employees of such employers shall have the right to be heard through their representatives in such court upon all questions affecting the terms and conditions of their employment; and no reduction of wages shall be made by such receivers without the authority of the court therefor, after notice to such employees, said notice to be given not less than twenty days before the hearing upon the receivers' petition or application, and to be posted upon all customary bulletin boards along or upon the railway or in the customary places on the premises of other employers covered by this Act.

SEC. 10. That each member of the board of arbitration created under the provisions of this Act shall receive such compensation as may be fixed by the Board of Mediation and Conciliation, together with his traveling and other necessary expenses. The sum of $25,000, or so much thereof as may be necessary, is hereby appropriated, to be immediately available and to continue available until the close of the fiscal year ending June thirtieth, nineteen hundred and fourteen, for the necessary and proper expenses incurred in connection with any arbitration or with the carrying on of the work of mediation and conciliation, including per diem, traveling, and other necessary expenses of members or employees of boards of arbitration and rent in the District of Columbia, furniture, office fixtures and supplies, books, salaries, traveling expenses, and other necessary expenses of members or employees of the Board of Mediation and Conciliation, to be approved by the chairman of said board and audited by the proper accounting officers of the Treasury.

SEC. 11. There shall be a Commissioner of Mediation and Conciliation, who shall be appointed by the President, by and with the advice and consent of the Senate, and whose salary shall be $7,500 per annum, who shall hold his office for a term of seven years and until a successor qualifies, and who shall be removable by the President only for misconduct in office. The President shall also designate not more than two other officials of the Government who have been appointed by and with the advice and consent of the Senate, and the officials thus designated, together with the Commissioner of Mediation and Conciliation, shall constitute a board to be known as the United States Board of Mediation and Conciliation.

There shall also be an Assistant Commissioner of Mediation and Conciliation, who shall be appointed by the President, by and with the advice and consent of the Senate, and whose salary shall be $5,000 per annum. In the absence of the Commissioner of Mediation and Conciliation, or when that office shall become vacant, the assistant commissioner shall exercise the functions and perform the duties of that office. Under the direction of the Commissioner of Mediation and Conciliation, the assistant commissioner shall assist in the work of mediation and conciliation and when acting alone in any case he shall have the right to take acknowledgments, receive agreements of arbitration, and cause the notices in writing to be served upon the arbitrators chosen by the respective parties to the controversy, as provided for in section five of this Act.

The Act of June first, eighteen hundred and ninety-eight, relating to the mediation and arbitration of controversies between railway companies and certain classes of their employees is hereby repealed: *Provided,* That any agreement of arbitration which, at the time of the passage of this Act, shall have been executed in accordance with the provisions of said Act of June first, eighteen hundred and ninety-eight, shall be governed by the provisions of said Act of June first, eighteen hundred and ninety-eight, and the proceedings thereunder shall be conducted in accordance with the provisions of said Act.

Approved July 15, 1913.

APPENDIX II

REPORT OF THE COMMISSION ON INDUSTRIAL RELATIONS

The report of Mr. Basil M. Manly, Director of Research and Investigation, contained the following statement and recommendations with reference to agencies of mediation, investigation, and arbitration.[1]

The result of the very extensive investigations which have been made regarding the agencies for mediation and arbitration in this country and abroad have been embodied in the plan for legislation which is attached hereto. The plan as presented is limited to a National System, but it is recommended that the State legislatures should enact legislation along the same general lines. The general principles which have governed in drawing up this plan may be stated as follows:

---

[1] Final Report of the Commission on Industrial Relations, 1915, pp. 194–201.

APPENDIX II

1. The Mediation Commission should be independent of, and definitely divorced from, every other department of the State or Federal Government. Its only power grows out of its impartiality and this can not be secured if it is subordinate to any other body whose sympathies either with labor or with capital can be questioned.
2. Mediation should be entrusted to a person as far as possible distinct from those who act as arbitrators or appoint arbitrators.
3. The office of mediator should be placed beyond the suspicion that the office is being used as a reward for party services.
4. The mediator should appoint his own subordinates.
5. It is desirable in the event of the failure of mediation by an official mediator, that the parties should be asked to consent to the appointment of a Board of Mediation and Investigation consisting of three persons, one selected by each party and the third by these two. Such a board, it appears, would be able to secure an agreement in many cases where the mediator fails. These boards should have power to summon witnesses and compel the production of papers. In the event that the board could not

secure an agreement during the investigation, it should be empowered to make a public report stating the terms on which, in its judgment, the parties should settle.

6. In those cases in which the parties are unable to agree on the third member of the Board of Mediation and Investigation, he should be appointed in the State Systems by the State Board of Arbitration, and in the National System by the mediators, from a list prepared in advance by an Advisory Board, consisting of ten representatives of employers' associations and ten representatives of trade unions.

7. National Boards of Mediation and Investigation are to be formed only in disputes involving interstate commerce and in those cases in which the legislature or the executive of a State has requested the intervention of the Federal Government.

8. The Secretary of Labor, or in the States the official, bureau or commission which is created for the protection of the workers, should be empowered to appear before the Board of Mediation and Investigation, when it is holding public hearings, either at the request of the board as *amicus curiae*, in the ascertainment of facts regarding labor conditions, or, if ap-

APPENDIX II

pealed to, as the spokesman for the employees in the presentation of their case.

PROPOSED PLAN OF A NATIONAL SYSTEM OF MEDIATION, INVESTIGATION AND ARBITRATION

ORGANIZATION

1. Scope of Authority.

The National Mediation Commission should be given exclusive authority to intervene, under the conditions hereinafter defined, in all industrial disputes involving any corporation, firm, or establishment except public service establishments, which is engaged in interstate commerce or whose products enter into interstate or foreign commerce.

This provision differentiates its functions from those of the Mediation Commission existing at present under the Newlands Act. It is considered desirable for the present to provide for the existence of the two commissions, at least until the proposed commission has been thoroughly tested. It is believed to be wise, however, to provide for their close coöperation from the very beginning, with the idea that they will ultimately be consolidated.

APPENDIX II

It will be noted that this provision also will have the effect of supplanting the mediation powers which are now vested in the Department of Labor. There is no desire to criticise or belittle the past activities of the mediators operating under the Department of Labor, for such criticism is absolutely unwarranted. It is also freely admitted that the Department of Labor has not had either the time or the resources necessary for the proper development of this function. The proposal is made, however, primarily upon three grounds which seem to be sound and, in fact, compelling: First, the function of mediation depends absolutely upon the permanent assurance of impartiality. The Department of Labor was created to represent the interests of labor and it seems not only inevitable but desirable and proper that the Secretary of Labor should always be drawn from the ranks of organized labor. The function of mediation may be administered with absolute impartiality under any particular Secretary, or even under every Secretary, and yet it seems impossible, even under such conditions, to create that absolute assurance of impartiality which is the prime essential. Second, it is the prerogative and duty of the Department of Labor to act, aggressively if need be, for the protection

185

of the workers at all times, and to utilize every resource at its command to give them that protection. The Department must necessarily be greatly impeded in such frankly partisan action, it would seem, if it must at the same time preserve either the substance or the shadow of impartiality in carrying out its function of mediation. Third, in the bitterest disputes, where the public interest most strongly demands intervention, mediation is seldom successful, and a stage is quickly reached where the most vital necessity is for the full and exact facts regarding the dispute, in order that public opinion may be intelligently formed and directed. Experience has shown that such facts can best be secured fully, quickly, and effectively through the medium of public inquiry. This means that the inquiring body must have power to summon witnesses, compel the production of books and papers, and compel testimony, or the proceeding is worse than a farce. It may be regarded as certain that such powers will never be entrusted to the Department of Labor.

2. Membership.

The members of the Mediation Commission should be appointed by the President with the advice and consent of the Senate. The members should represent in proper balance the interests of employers, employees, and the public. The members should serve for terms of six years.

3. Advisory Board.

The President of the United States should designate an equal number of leading organizations of employers and leading organizations of employees to appoint representatives to act as an advisory body to the President, to Congress, and to the Mediation Commission. This body, designated hereinafter the Advisory Board, should give advice regarding the duties of the commission, the administration of its affairs and the selection of mediators, and be empowered to make recommendations regarding legislation. The Advisory Board should also prepare lists of persons who may be called upon to serve on boards of arbitration and on boards of mediation and investigation. The Advisory Board should be called together at least once a year by the Chairman of the Mediation Commission; it should have an organization independent of the commission and elect its own chairman and secretary.

The members of the Advisory Board should be paid traveling and other necessary expenses and such compensation as may be determined upon. Provision should be made for the removal of members by the organizations which they represent.

4. Subordinate Officers and Assistants.

The Mediation Commission should have power to appoint, remove at pleasure, and fix the compensation of a secretary (and a limited number of clerks). The appointment of other officers and assistants, such as mediators, examiners, investigators, technical assessors, experts, disbursing officer, clerks, and other employees, should be subject to the Civil Service rules. But arrangements should be made to have the examination include experience and other proper qualifications, and to give the Mediation Commission power to examine all candidates orally.

POWERS, DUTIES, AND JURISDICTION

5. In Interstate Commerce.

(a) Mediation: Whenever a controversy concerning conditions of employment arises between employer and employees engaged in interstate commerce other than public service corporations, either party should be able to apply to the chairman of the Mediation Commission for its services in the bringing about of an amicable adjustment of the controversy. Or, the chairman of the commission should be authorized to offer, on his own initiative, the services of the mediators of the commission. If efforts to bring about an amicable adjustment through mediation should be unsuccessful, the commission should at once, if possible, induce the parties to submit their differences to arbitration.

(b) Arbitration: Procedure should be similar to that outlined in the Newlands Act. If it is necessary for the Mediation Commission to appoint arbitrators, they should be taken from a list prepared by the Advisory Board.

(c) Boards of Mediation and Investigation: If the parties to the controversy can not be induced to arbitrate, and if the controversy should threaten to interrupt the business of employers and employees to the detriment of the public interest, the commission should be authorized to request the two parties to consent to the creation of a Board of Mediation and Investigation. If the consent of the parties to the controversy is secured, the commission shall form such a board. Of the three members of the board, one should be selected by the employers, one by the employees, and a third on the recommendation of the members so chosen. If either side fails to recommend a member, he should be appointed by the commission. If after a stated time the third member is not recommended, the commission should select him. Appointments to boards of mediation and investigation shall be made by the commission from a list prepared for this purpose by the Advisory board. The Board of Mediation and Investigation should offer its friendly offices in bringing about a settlement of the dispute through mediation. If mediation should not be successful and if the parties to the controversy refuse to arbitrate, this board should have power to make an investigation of the controversy, and should be required to submit to the commission a full report thereon, including recommendations for its settlement. The commission should be empowered to give this report and recommendations adequate publicity.

(d) Powers to Secure Evidence: A Board of Mediation and Investigation should have power to administer oaths, to subpena and compel the attendance and testimony of witnesses, and the production of books, papers, documents, etc., and to conduct hearings and investigations, and to exercise such other similar powers as might be necessary. It should not have power to prohibit, or to impose penalties for, strikes or lockouts.

APPENDIX II

6. Not in Interstate Commerce.

It should be provided that the commission, or a Board of Mediation and Investigation created by it, may exercise the foregoing powers except the compulsory powers under subdivision "d" of Proposal 5, for settling industrial controversies between parties not engaged in interstate commerce, if they are requested to do so by the Governor or legislature of a State, or by the mayor, council, or commission of a municipality.

7. The Secretary of Labor and the Secretary of Commerce should be authorized to bring to the attention of the commission any dispute in which the intervention of the commission seems desirable. The Secretary of Labor, or such officer as he may designate, should also be authorized to appear before any Board of Mediation and Investigation, either at the request of the board as *amicus curiae* for the ascertainment of facts regarding labor conditions, or, if appealed to, as a spokesman for the employees in the presentation of their case.

COÖPERATION

8. Coöperation with State and Local Authorities.

The commission should be authorized and directed to coöperate with state, local, and territorial authorities and similar departments of foreign countries which deal with the adjustment of industrial disputes.

9. Coöperation with Other Federal Agencies.

The commission should, as far as practicable, coördinate its activities and coöperate with other Federal departments in the performance of their duties.

The report of Mr. Manly as a whole was signed by Chairman Frank P. Walsh, and Commissioners John B. Lennon, James O'Connell, and Austin B. Garretson. All of those signing the report of Mr. Manly wrote also supplemental statements which contain references to the section of the report relating to agencies of mediation, investigation, and arbitration. The sections of these supplemental reports dealing with the subject are contained in Appendix III.

APPENDIX III

REPORT OF THE COMMISSION ON INDUS-
TRIAL RELATIONS

The supplemental statement of Commissioners John B. Lennon and James O'Connell contains the following passage relating to the subject: [1]

EXTENT OF UNREST

The principal duty imposed, under the law creating the commission, was to seek to ascertain the causes of industrial unrest and offer such recommendations as we believe might alleviate that unrest. There can be no question but that unrest exists, in some instances, to an alarming extent. Thousands and tens of thousands of our people feel that they are deprived, under existing conditions in industry, of an opportunity to secure for themselves and their families a standard of living commensurate with the best ideals of manhood, womanhood, and childhood. They re-

---

[1] Final Report of the Commission on Industrial Relations, 1915, pp. 283–286.

193

sent the fact that the existing system of the distribution of wealth creates at one end of our industrial scale a few multi-millionaires and at the other end thousands and tens of thousands of men, women, and children who are at all times in a situation where they are uncertain as to where their next meal will come from. Hungry, poorly clothed, and without the opportunities that a fully rounded life requires, they become filled with a sullen resentment that bodes no good for the future of our Republic.

We have found men and women who are inclined to ascribe this condition to the fact that the Government exercises no power of mandatory character to prevent strikes and lockouts. Many have been the propositions submitted to us for compulsory arbitration or, at least, compulsory investigation with power to recommend a settlement. Some have proposed an elaborate machinery to be set up by the general Government, and of a similar character by the States, providing for conciliation, mediation, arbitration, and investigation, all of which, while without definite compulsory features, establish a legal machinery that must of necessity exercise an influence in that direction.

The plan for the creation of an industrial com-

APPENDIX III

mission, both National and State, proposes to assign to a commission of three members the administration of all labor laws of either State or Nation, giving to them powers far in excess of those exercised by the President of the United States, or the Governor of any State. This we believe to be Bureaucracy run mad, and a subversion of Democracy dangerous to the civil and social liberty of all citizens. We hold that all power should be in the final analysis with the people, and we therefore, dissent from any such plan.

NEW GOVERNMENTAL MACHINERY UNWISE

The activities of such a commission supplemented by the proposed advisory committees of employers and labor representatives would be so balanced as to prevent substantial progress, and tend to perpetuate present conditions. Such a plan conceives of labor and capital as static forces and of the relations between them as always to remain unchanging.

We believe that the work now being done by the Department of Labor in industry generally, and by the Board of Mediation and Conciliation, dealing with interstate public utilities, is better than any that could be expected of any additional

APPENDIX III

board that has been suggested to this commission. We believe that the Department of Labor, with further experience and larger appropriations, will develop a high state of efficiency in adjusting labor disputes that are capable of being adjusted by any one other than the parties directly interested, and will adequately carry on the work provided by the law creating the Department of Labor, to wit:

SECTION 1. The purpose of the Department of Labor shall be to foster, promote, and develop the welfare of the wage earners in the United States, to improve their working conditions, and to advance their opportunities for profitable employment.

SECTION 8. The Secretary of Labor shall have power to act as mediator and to appoint commissioners of conciliation in labor disputes whenever in his judgment the interests of industrial peace require it to be done.

We favor the extension of the Newlands Act to cover all employees engaged in interstate commerce, such as the railroad telegraphers, the shop and track men employed by railroads, the employees of express companies, of the Pullman Company, of commercial telegraph and telephone companies, and other public utilities performing interstate service that, in the interest of the Nation, must be continuous.

The evidence submitted to this commission is substantially to the effect that where trade union organization exists among the workers, there, at the same time, exists the least amount of industrial unrest of a character that is dangerous to the peace and welfare of our nation. It is true that the union men and women are not satisfied with their conditions; they are not, however, despondent as to the possibility of securing better conditions; they know what the unions have accomplished, and they have an abiding faith that their further desires can be attained.

Instead of any elaborate machinery for the prevention of strikes or lockouts we are convinced, from the testimony gathered by this commission, that the most effectual course that can be pursued to bring about general contentment among our people, based upon a humane standard of living, is the promotion of labor organization. The most casual investigator will soon discover that in those lines of industry where organization of labor is the strongest, there is the least danger of industrial revolt that would endanger the fundamental principles of our Government and the maintenance of a nation with respect for law and order. Where organization is lacking, dangerous discontent is found on every hand; low wages and long hours prevail; exploitation in every direction is practiced; the people become sullen, have no regard for law or government and are, in reality, a latent volcano, as dangerous to society as are the volcanoes of nature to the landscape surrounding them.

The supplemental statement of Commissioner Austin B. Garretson contains the following passages relating to the subject: [1]

My signature is appended to the Report of Mr. Basil M. Manly, Director of Research and Investigation of the United States Commission on Industrial Relations, submitted to the commission and transmitted herewith, as to the findings of fact contained therein.

I am in general agreement with the recommendations contained in that Report except as to the formation of the system of State and Federal Commissions and a Federal Industrial Council.

On this recommendation I neither approve nor condemn. But out of regard for the opinion of

---

[1] Final Report of the Commission on Industrial Relations, 1915, p. 291.

the great body of intra-state labor most directly
affected, I dissent. . . .

I am favorable to the extension of the provisions of the Newlands Act to all classes of interstate employees who can constitutionally be
brought under its provisions and would favor the
enlargement of the body administering it to meet
the added responsibilities which would thereby be
placed upon it, but limiting the powers thereof to
the settlement of industrial disagreements and to
the gathering of information germane to their mission.

I favor the creation of state commissions, similarly constituted and acting in corelation and understanding with the Federal Board.

I heartily concur with the Report of Commissioners Lennon and O'Connell except on those
points where disagreement is herein noted. I dissent in whole from the report rendered by Commissioner J. R. Commons.

*The supplemental statement of Chairman
Frank P. Walsh contains the following passage
relating to the subject:* [1]

Although I have signed the report prepared

---

[1] Final Report of the Commission on Industrial Relations, 1915, p. 302.

APPENDIX III

by Mr. Basil M. Manly, Director of Research and Investigation, because I believe it represents an unassailable statement of the existing industrial situation, because it fully complies with the requirements of the Act of Congress creating the commission, and because the recommendations are as a whole wise and necessary for the welfare of the Nation, I, nevertheless, desire to record my dissent on the following points—

1. The recommendation for new administrative machinery for mediation and arbitration in the form of a special commission. I believe that the commission created by the Newlands Act, and the Department of Labor, if their powers are enlarged and they are adequately supported, will be fully able to deal with the situation. . . .

APPENDIX IV

REPORT OF THE COMMISSION ON INDUSTRIAL RELATIONS

The report of Commissioners John R. Commons and Florence J. Harriman contains the following recommendations relating to mediation, investigation, and arbitration.[1]

MEDIATION AND MINIMUM WAGE

The Industrial Commission (State or Federal) shall appoint, remove and fix the compensation of a chief mediator of industrial disputes. The chief mediator to hold his position until removed by the Industrial Commission and to appoint such assistants as may be needed, and to fix their compensation with the approval of the Industrial Commission. He should appoint temporary mediators for special cases, without requiring them to give up their private business or offices.

The chief mediator and all assistant mediators

---

[1] Final Report of the Commission on Industrial Relations, 1915, pp. 364–366, 376–377.

201

APPENDIX IV

to be selected from an eligible list prepared by the Civil Service Commission on a nonassembled examination, with the assistance of the Industrial Commission and the Advisory Council.

The chief mediator and his staff to have no powers whatever of compulsory testimony and to be prohibited from arbitrating any dispute, from making any public recommendation, or from revealing in any way, directly or indirectly, any information which they may have secured from any parties relative to an industrial dispute. Any violation to be sufficient ground for immediate removal by the Industrial Commission. The powers of the mediators to be those solely of voluntary mediation or conciliation but the chief mediator shall offer his services in confidence to both sides of a dispute which, in his judgment, is of public importance.

The chief mediator and his staff to be wholly independent of the Industrial Commission, except as to appointment and removal, to the extent that they be prohibited from reporting any facts or recommendations whatever to the Industrial Commission or any other authority, relative to the merits of any industrial dispute.

In case the mediator is unable to secure an agreement through conciliation, he shall recommend arbitration to both parties, and if both consent to abide by the decision of arbitrators he shall proceed to assist them in selecting a board of arbitration in any way, and consisting of any number of members, that both sides may agree upon. If agreement is not reached within a specified time on the third party to the board of mediation, the chief mediator shall appoint the same.

In case both parties do not consent to arbitration the mediator shall recommend the appointment of a board of mediation and investigation, which shall have power to make public its findings and recommendations, but such recommendations shall not be binding on any person. If both parties shall consent to such a board the mediator shall assist them in creating the same, and shall appoint the third member if the parties can not agree on the same within a specified number of days.

In case both parties accept either a board of arbitration or a board of mediation and investigation, such board, as the case may be, shall have power of compelling testimony. The "Newlands Act" and the Department of Labor act should be so amended that all mediation and conciliation, whether on railways or in other industries, shall be consolidated under the mediator of the Federal Industrial Commission. The Federal Commission should coöperate with State mediators.

In the case of women and children, minimum wage boards should be created by the state industrial commissions.

The foregoing recommendation is intended to provide for strictly "voluntary" methods of mediation and arbitration. When engaged in this branch of its work the commission is not only prohibited from using its compulsory powers, but its mediation work is so rigidly separated from its other work that it can not even be suspected of using the coercive power of Government to favor either side. The mediator and his staff are to be strictly confidential advisors to the opposing interests, without the power of Government, or even the threat of using that power, to coerce either side of a collective dispute. If coercion is used in the form of " compulsory testimony" it is only with the previous voluntary consent of both sides. . . .

After considering all forms of Governmental compulsion in collective disputes and even admitting their partial success in other countries, we conclude that, on the whole, in this country, as much can be accomplished in the long run by strictly voluntary methods as by compulsory methods of avoiding strikes and lockouts. It can not be expected that strikes and lockouts can be abolished altogether. Even countries with compulsory systems have not succeeded in preventing all of them. In our country, the voluntary method in collective bargaining avoids the much more serious evil of discrediting the agencies of Government which must be looked to for impartial enforcement of laws affecting the individual labor contract. It is to the enactment and enforcement of laws protecting laborers as individuals that we must look for the removal of underlying causes of industrial unrest and for the eventual reduction of strikes that now spring from the cumulative abuses that individuals suffer without other effective remedies. But the removal of these abuses can not be accomplished without the efficient and nonpartisan administration of laws, and this is the main purport of our recommendation for industrial commissions to regulate the individual labor contract.

The report of Commissioners Commons and Harriman was signed also by Commissioners Harris Weinstock, S. Thurston Ballard, and Richard H. Aishton. Commissioners Weinstock, Ballard, and Aishton made also a joint supplemental re-

APPENDIX IV

port in which the following passage relating to the subject occurs:[1]

We concur in the report prepared by Commissioner Commons, dissenting, however, on the two following points, and supplementing it by certain other findings and recommendations following herewith. . . .

Second. We further dissent from said report in its limitation of public inquiry in labor disputes only to cases where both sides invite such inquiry. We believe that in the public interest there are times when compulsion in labor disputes is thoroughly justified. We feel, with organized labor, that there should be no restriction put upon the right to strike, realizing as we do, that the strike is the only weapon which, in the interest of labor, can be effectively and legally used to aid in bettering its conditions. We feel, also, that there should be no restriction placed upon the employer in his right to declare a lockout in order to better protect what he regards as his interest, and we therefore would not favor any plan that would inflict penalties upon the worker or upon the employer for declaring a strike or lockout.

---

[1] Final Report of the Commission on Industrial Relations, 1915, pp. 407, 409–411.

APPENDIX IV

Where the two sides to a labor controversy are fairly well balanced in strength, the winning side must depend, in the last analysis, upon the support of public opinion. Public opinion, therefore, becomes a most important factor in the interest of industrial peace. Such public opinion, however, to be of value, must be enlightened. Under prevailing conditions this is almost impossible. All that the public is now able to get, as a rule, are garbled and *ex parte* statements, more or less misleading and unreliable, which simply tend to confuse the public mind.

Where strikes and lockouts take place on a large scale, and more especially in connection with public utilities, the public inevitably becomes a third party to the issue, in that it has more at stake than both parties to the dispute combined. For example, if the street railways of a large city are tied up, the loss to the railway companies in the way of revenue, and to the workers in the way of wages, is great, but this loss becomes insignificant compared with the loss inflicted upon the rest of the community, to say nothing of the annoyance, inconvenience, and menace to life and property, which not infrequently occur in such industrial disputes. The public, therefore, as the third party to the issue, is justified in demanding that an investigation take place, and that the facts be ascertained and presented in an impartial spirit to the general public, so that ways and means may be found of adjudicating the dispute or of throwing the influence of a properly informed public opinion on the side which has the right in its favor.

We, therefore, earnestly recommend that in the case of public utilities, the proposed industrial commission shall not only have power to mediate and conciliate, but also, at the request of either side to a dispute, or upon the initiative of the commission itself, should have the power, all voluntary methods having failed, to undertake a compulsory public inquiry when, in the discretion of the commission, public interest demands it; that it be given the fullest powers to summon witnesses, place them under oath, demand books and documents, all with a view of ascertaining the underlying causes of the dispute and the issues involved, to the end of making recommendations that, in the judgment of the board of inquiry, consisting of three members, one to be chosen by each side and the third to be chosen by these two, would be a fair and reasonable settlement of the points in dispute. It being understood, however, that neither side is obliged to accept such recommendations, but may continue to strike or lock out, as the case may be. Meanwhile, however, the public will have ascertained in the most reliable way, the issues involved, the facts as they have been found by the board of inquiry, and the basis upon which a fair settlement can be established, thus enabling the public more intelligently to throw its support where it rightfully belongs.

(1)

American Labor: From Conspiracy to Collective Bargaining

AN ARNO PRESS/NEW YORK TIMES COLLECTION

SERIES I

Abbott, Edith.
Women in Industry. 1913.

Aveling, Edward B. and Eleanor M. Aveling.
Working Class Movement in America. 1891.

Beard, Mary.
The American Labor Movement. 1939.

Blankenhorn, Heber.
The Strike for Union. 1924.

Blum, Solomon.
Labor Economics. 1925.

Brandeis, Louis D. and Josephine Goldmark.
Women in Industry. 1907. New introduction by Leon Stein and
Philip Taft.

Brooks, John Graham.
American Syndicalism. 1913.

Butler, Elizabeth Beardsley.
Women and the Trades. 1909.

Byington, Margaret Frances.
Homestead: The Household of A Mill Town. 1910.

Carroll, Mollie Ray.
Labor and Politics. 1923.

Coleman, McAlister.
Men and Coal. 1943.

Coleman, J. Walter.
The Molly Maguire Riots: Industrial Conflict in the Pennsylvania Coal Region. 1936.

Commons, John R.
Industrial Goodwill. 1919.

Commons, John R.
Industrial Government. 1921.

Dacus, Joseph A.
Annals of the Great Strikes. 1877.

Dealtry, William.
The Laborer: A Remedy for his Wrongs. 1869.

Douglas, Paul H., Curtis N. Hitchcock and Willard E. Atkins, editors.
The Worker in Modern Economic Society. 1923.

Eastman, Crystal.
Work Accidents and the Law. 1910.

Ely, Richard T.
The Labor Movement in America. 1890. New Introduction by Leon Stein and Philip Taft.

Feldman, Herman.
Problems in Labor Relations. 1937.

Fitch, John Andrew.
The Steel Worker. 1910.

Furniss, Edgar S. and Laurence Guild.
Labor Problems. 1925.

Gladden, Washington.
Working People and Their Employers. 1885.

Gompers, Samuel.
Labor and the Common Welfare. 1919.

Hardman, J. B. S., editor.
American Labor Dynamics. 1928.

Higgins, George G.
Voluntarism in Organized Labor, 1930-40. 1944.

Hiller, Ernest T.
The Strike. 1928.

Hollander, Jacob S. and George E. Barnett.
Studies in American Trade Unionism. 1906. New Introduction by
 Leon Stein and Philip Taft.

Jelley, Symmes M.
The Voice of Labor. 1888.

Jones, Mary.
Autobiography of Mother Jones. 1925.

Kelley, Florence.
Some Ethical Gains Through Legislation. 1905.

LaFollette, Robert M., editor.
The Making of America: Labor. 1906.

Lane, Winthrop D.
Civil War in West Virginia. 1921.

Lauck, W. Jett and Edgar Sydenstricker.
Conditions of Labor in American Industries. 1917.

Leiserson, William M.
Adjusting Immigrant and Industry. 1924.

Lescohier, Don D.
Knights of St. Crispin. 1910.

Levinson, Edward.
I Break Strikes. The Technique of Pearl L. Bergoff. 1935.

Lloyd, Henry Demarest.
Men, The Workers. Compiled by Anne Whithington and
 Caroline Stallbohen. 1909. New Introduction by Leon Stein
 and Philip Taft.

Lorwin, Louis (Louis Levine).
The Women's Garment Workers. 1924.

Markham, Edwin, Ben B. Lindsay and George Creel.
Children in Bondage. 1914.

Marot, Helen.
American Labor Unions. 1914.

Mason, Alpheus T.
Organized Labor and the Law. 1925.

Newcomb, Simon.
A Plain Man's Talk on the Labor Question. 1886. New Introduction
  by Leon Stein and Philip Taft.

Price, George Moses.
The Modern Factory: Safety, Sanitation and Welfare. 1914.

Randall, John Herman Jr.
Problem of Group Responsibility to Society. 1922.

Rubinow, I. M.
Social Insurance. 1913.

Saposs, David, editor.
Readings in Trade Unionism. 1926.

Slichter, Sumner H.
Union Policies and Industrial Management. 1941.

Socialist Publishing Society.
The Accused and the Accusers. 1887.

Stein, Leon and Philip Taft, editors.
The Pullman Strike. 1894-1913. New Introduction by the editors.

Stein, Leon and Philip Taft, editors.
Religion, Reform, and Revolution: Labor Panaceas in the Nineteenth
  Century. 1969. New Introduction by the editors.

Stein, Leon and Philip Taft, editors.
Wages, Hours, and Strikes: Labor Panaceas in the Twentieth Century.
  1969. New introduction by the editors.

Swinton, John.
A Momentous Question: The Respective Attitudes of Labor and Capital. 1895. New Introduction by Leon Stein and Philip Taft.

Tannenbaum, Frank.
The Labor Movement. 1921.

Tead, Ordway.
Instincts in Industry. 1918.

Vorse, Mary Heaton.
Labor's New Millions. 1938.

Witte, Edwin Emil.
The Government in Labor Disputes. 1932.

Wright, Carroll D.
The Working Girls of Boston. 1889.

Wyckoff, Veitrees J.
Wage Policies of Labor Organizations in a Period of Industrial Depression. 1926.

Yellen, Samuel.
American Labor Struggles. 1936.

SERIES II

Allen, Henry J.
The Party of the Third Part: The Story of the Kansas Industrial Relations Court. 1921. *Including* **The Kansas Court of Industrial Relations Law** (1920) by Samuel Gompers.

Baker, Ray Stannard.
The New Industrial Unrest. 1920.

Barnett, George E. & David A. McCabe.
Mediation, Investigation and Arbitration in Industrial Disputes. 1916.

Barns, William E., editor.
The Labor Problem. 1886.

Bing, Alexander M.
War-Time Strikes and Their Adjustment. 1921.

Brooks, Robert R. R.
When Labor Organizes. 1937.

Calkins, Clinch.
Spy Overhead: The Story of Industrial Espionage. 1937.

Cooke, Morris Llewellyn & Philip Murray.
Organized Labor and Production. 1940.

Creamer, Daniel & Charles W. Coulter.
Labor and the Shut-Down of the Amoskeag Textile Mills. 1939.

Glocker, Theodore W.
The Government of American Trade Unions. 1913.

Gompers, Samuel.
Labor and the Employer. 1920.

Grant, Luke.
The National Erectors' Association and the International Association of Bridge and Structural Ironworkers. 1915.

Haber, William.
Industrial Relations in the Building Industry. 1930.

Henry, Alice.
Women and the Labor Movement. 1923.

Herbst, Alma.
The Negro in the Slaughtering and Meat-Packing Industry in Chicago. 1932.

[Hicks, Obediah.]
Life of Richard F. Trevellick. 1896.

Hillquit, Morris, Samuel Gompers & Max J. Hayes.
The Double Edge of Labor's Sword: Discussion and Testimony on Socialism and Trade-Unionism Before the Commission on Industrial Relations. 1914. New Introduction by Leon Stein and Philip Taft.

Jensen, Vernon H.
Lumber and Labor. 1945.

Kampelman, Max M.
The Communist Party vs. the C.I.O. 1957.

Kingsbury, Susan M., editor.
Labor Laws and Their Enforcement. By Charles E. Persons, Mabel Parton, Mabelle Moses & Three "Fellows." 1911.

McCabe, David A.
The Standard Rate in American Trade Unions. 1912.

Mangold, George Benjamin.
Labor Argument in the American Protective Tariff Discussion. 1908.

Millis, Harry A., editor.
How Collective Bargaining Works. 1942.

Montgomery, Royal E.
Industrial Relations in the Chicago Building Trades. 1927.

Oneal, James.
The Workers in American History. 3rd edition, 1912.

Palmer, Gladys L.
Union Tactics and Economic Change: A Case Study of Three Philadelphia Textile Unions. 1932.

Penny, Virginia.
How Women Can Make Money: Married or Single, In all Branches of the Arts and Sciences, Professions, Trades, Agricultural and Mechanical Pursuits. 1870. New Introduction by Leon Stein and Philip Taft.

Penny, Virginia.
Think and Act: A Series of Articles Pertaining to Men and Women, Work and Wages. 1869.

Pickering, John.
The Working Man's Political Economy. 1847.

Ryan, John A.
A Living Wage. 1906.

Savage, Marion Dutton.
Industrial Unionism in America. 1922.

Simkhovitch, Mary Kingsbury.
The City Worker's World in America. 1917.

Spero, Sterling Denhard.
The Labor Movement in a Government Industry: A Study of Employee Organization in the Postal Service. 1927.

Stein, Leon and Philip Taft, editors.
Labor Politics: Collected Pamphlets. 2 vols. 1836-1932. New Introduction by the editors.

Stein, Leon and Philip Taft, editors.
The Management of Workers: Selected Arguments. 1917-1956. New Introduction by the editors.

Stein, Leon and Philip Taft, editors.
Massacre at Ludlow: Four Reports. 1914-1915. New Introduction by the editors.

Stein, Leon and Philip Taft, editors.
Workers Speak: Self-Portraits. 1902-1906. New Introduction by the editors.

Stolberg, Benjamin.
The Story of the CIO. 1938.

Taylor, Paul S.
The Sailors' Union of the Pacific. 1923.

U.S. Commission on Industrial Relations.
Efficiency Systems and Labor. 1916. New Introduction by Leon Stein and Philip Taft.

Walker, Charles Rumford.
American City: A Rank-and-File History. 1937.

Walling, William English.
American Labor and American Democracy. 1926.

Williams, Whiting.
What's on the Worker's Mind: By One Who Put on Overalls to Find Out. 1920.

Wolman, Leo.
The Boycott in American Trade Unions. 1916.

Ziskind, David.
One Thousand Strikes of Government Employees. 1940.